Free Stuff
FOR
Quilters
ON THE
INTERNET

Judy Heim and Gloria Hansen

Copyright © 1998 Judy Heim and Gloria Hansen
Developmental Editor: Barbara Konzak Kuhn
Technical Editor: Vera Tobin
Cover & Book Design: Christina Jarumay
Front Cover Illustration: Alan McCorkle
Illustrations on page 11 and back cover: Christina Jarumay

Library of Congress Cataloging-in-Publication Data
Heim, Judy.
    Free stuff for quilters on the Internet/ Judy Heim and Gloria Hansen.
    p.   cm.
    Includes index.
    ISBN 1-57120-054-1
    1. Quilting--Computer network resources--Directories. 2. Internet (Computer network)--Directories. 3. Web sites--Directories. 4. Free material--Directories. I. Hansen, Gloria. II. Title.
TT835.H3867   1998
746.46'025--dc21   98-24728
                                                                CIP

Published by C&T Publishing, Inc.
P.O. Box 1456
Lafayette, California 94549

Printed in the United States
10 9 8 7 6 5 4 3 2 1

DEDICATION

We dedicate this book to the spirit that inspires quilters and other craftspeople to share so freely of themselves, their skills, and their friendship on the Web. By sharing we open new worlds in the hearts and minds of others, including strangers we may never meet. We also grow friendships that are irreplaceable—well, like our own!

Judy & Gloria

We hope *Free Stuff for Quilters on the Internet* will get you started exploring and enjoying the Web like many quilters are doing already. There are thousands of Web sites for quilters, and the number grows daily. We could not include them all in this book, although we would have liked to. We sifted and sorted and came up with those that we think offer valuable information to quilters. That doesn't mean there aren't many others out there that are equally illuminating and valuable. Also, because of the fluid nature of the Internet, it is inevitable that some of the Web sites listed may have moved or even vanished. Had we included only those Web sites that are sure to be around many moons from now, this book wouldn't be nearly as valuable. And, while you can find lots of free goodies on the Internet, you can learn more if you participate in quilting classes offered by your local quilt store. Quilt stores are excellent resources for quilting news, help, and advice. And they're just darn good places to meet other quilters, too!

Symbols in this book

 This icon signifies a bit of Judy-and-Gloria hard-earned wisdom—in other words, something we wished we knew when we first started cruising the Web.

 When you see this icon, read carefully—and don't make one of the same silly mistakes we have!

 This icon means that the Web site also sells products that relate to the information on their site.

Table of Contents

CHAPTER 1

Get Yourself on the Web!

Every seller of toothpaste and TV dinners has a Web site. Even ads for movies flash a Web address at the bottom of the screen. Does anyone actually tap into these sites? Sometimes we wonder.

You can find just about anyone and anything on the Internet, that maze of haphazardly connected computers that spans the globe, linking even ships at sea to the cyberspace soup. A half-dozen years ago the Internet was an obscure network tying universities and government labs. Now even the Chinese government has its own Web site (remember China's outrage when news of the Tiananmen Square uprising leaked from its universities to the world via the Internet and they practically banned PCs?). Philippine senators have their own Web sites where they entertain comments from constituents, and you can tap into Web sites in the Czech Republic to buy watches.

In just five short years the Internet has become newsstand, global town square, and encyclopedia at once. Have a question about a rare species of bird? Type it into one of the many Internet search engines and you'll have your answer in a flash, courtesy of computers that may be on the other side of the earth. Need advice on how to buy a quilt frame? The Internet can fill you in on that too. Answers to almost anything can be found on the Net.

In fact, you can find almost anything on there, period. From potato salad recipes to stanzas of obscure religious hymns. From coffee klatches of antique dealers to support groups for whatever ails you. From splashy Web sites for quilting celebrities like David Walker (**http://w3.one.net/~davidxix/.**) to humble home pages for Midwestern quilt guilds.

And yes, there are quilt patterns out there too. Thousands of them. There are also galleries of quilts that you can view on your computer.

There are articles on quilting that you can read.

There are things you can query, like fabric types and notions.

There is quilting advice—and advice, and advice, more than you can read in a lifetime.

And there are quilters you can swap e-mail with—tens of thousands of them, from countries around the world.

Just like the Internet transformed scientific research by allowing new ideas to cross over the planet, it is revolutionizing quilting by bringing together quilters and their imaginations at the speed of fiber optics.

That's what this book is about: how you can find and download some absolutely amazing things off the Internet, such as free patterns and advice, and in the process become wired, as they say.

❓ "IS STUFF REALLY FREE?" Why?

You're skeptical. No one gives you anything for free—not anything good, that is. Why should there be anything worthwhile available free online? Because companies put neat things on their Web sites so that you will tap in, and by that, be more apt to buy their products either online or in stores. And also because quilters are by nature generous free spirits. We enjoy sharing the fruits of our creativity as much as we enjoy being creative.

The only expense you'll bear by tapping into these Web sites to print free directions or patterns is the cost of your Internet access—the cost of your America Online subscription, for example, or the cost of your Internet service provider.

❓ "WHERE DO I SIGN UP?"

If you've never been on the Internet before, the best way to get started is to pop into your drive one of the free startup diskettes from America Online (**http://www.aol.com**). If you subscribe to any computer magazines, or have ever in your lifetime attached your address to anything computer-related, open your mailbox and an America Online disk will probably fall out. You can also get a startup CD-ROM by calling 800/827-6364, or have a friend download the software for you from the Web.

While you can use just about any computer to log onto the Internet in some fashion (even an original Apple II circa 1979), in order to view graphics you'll need a computer manufactured in at least the last 8 years. It's a misconception that you need the hottest computer in the store to be able to surf the Web (or design quilts for that matter).

Once you've installed the software and have connected to America Online, press Ctrl-K, or Command-K on a Mac, and type the keyword internet <enter> or web <enter>, and you're on the Internet.

Prodigy (**http://www.prodigy.com**) is also a good way to get started. You can get a free startup CD-ROM by calling 800/213-0992. You also use "go" words like internet and web to get you to the Net.

Once you feel comfortable online, you'll want to switch from America Online to a local Internet service. America Online can be slow, and in the evening, when every teenager in the world is logged on, you may get lots of busy signals if you try to log on. It's also easy to run up big bills on AOL.

The best way to shop for a local Internet service, or ISP, is to ask friends and neighbors for recommendations. TheList (**http://www.thelist.com**) offers a directory of ISPs around the country, searchable by area code.

Look for an ISP with a fast connection directly into the Internet's network backbone (ask for a T1 connection or better) and 56K bps local dial-up connections. Look for a flat monthly rate of about $20 for a goodly amount, or even more if you can afford unlimited Internet access. An ISP that gives you the ability to host a Web page is even better.

? "WHAT ABOUT GETTING INTERNET ACCESS THROUGH MY TV, OR CABLE?"

WebTVs or NetTVs are growing in popularity. These are fairly low cost (around $200) VCR-like units that let you surf the Web via your TV and an attached keyboard. Instead of an Internet service or America Online you connect via a special service usually run by the maker of your TV-Internet device. Cost is about $20 a month. There are drawbacks. The Internet just doesn't look as good on a TV screen as it does on a computer monitor. The connections can be slow, and it's hard to interact with the rest of the Internet. Worse, you can't use the software that everyone else is using (like the chat software). This is clearly a technology in its infancy.

While WebTVs connect to the Internet through a telephone line, there are also cable links to the Internet. Services like @Home and Time-Warner's Road Runner advertise Internet connections with speeds dozens of times that of a 28K bps modem on an old-fashioned phone line. You need a special cable modem (around $300). You also need a local cable operator that provides Internet hookups.

These services have been plagued with a high level of consumer dissatisfaction, however. Internet connect speeds aren't nearly as fast as the services brag. Upload speeds are especially slow. Because these services work by essentially transforming one's neighborhood into a wide-area network, like one linking a large company, there have been many reported instances of Web surfing neighbors reading the contents of each others' hard disks because of a Windows 95 file-sharing quirk.

For the time being, the most reliable links to the Internet remain America Online or an Internet service.

🔢 "WHAT SOFTWARE DO I NEED?"

To connect to the Internet through an ISP you need a Web browser like Netscape Navigator or Internet Explorer. If they're not already on your computer (most computers are sold with one or the other already installed) you can download them for free from Netscape's Web site (**http://www.netscape.com**) or Microsoft's (**http://www.microsoft.com**).

If you've never configured Internet software before, you'll need someone to help you, even if you're a computer genius (believe us, we know). Your ISP will (or should) give you directions on how to set up Windows 95 or the Macintosh OS to at least log on to their service.

But once you're connected, you're pretty much on your own. That's why we've put together this little tutorial.

Call Us Fuddy-Duddies If You Wish, But... Our favorite browsers are Netscape 3.0 and Internet Explorer 3.0. These are not the latest versions of these browsers, but they're quicker loading and less buggy than the current versions.

 ## ANATOMY OF A WEB BROWSER

In the old days you needed different sorts of software to accomplish different chores on the Internet: you needed mail software to send and receive e-mail; you needed a newsreader to read public discussions; you needed special software called FTP for "file download protocol" to download files to your computer. And you needed a browser to view (or browse through) the graphical portion of the Internet known as the Web.

Nowadays all those functions are built into Internet Explorer and Navigator. But the browsers' modular design makes some of their capabilities hard to find. Here's how to get around:

Note: The following directions are for Explorer 4.0 and Navigator 4.0 but, with the exception of the instructions for e-mail, most will work with previous versions of the browsers.

 ## HOW TO TAP INTO A WEB PAGE

To get to a Web page, type its address, also known as its URL, or Universal Resource Locator, into the Address: bar in Navigator, or the Location: bar in Internet Explorer.

(In older Web browsers you must preface the address with http: as in **http://www.jinnybeyer.com**, but in new browsers you can type simply **www.jinnybeyer.com**.)

Take note that the case of the letters is important (whether the letters are uppercase or lowercase).

You can also cut and paste URLs from other documents into the address or location bar. (Highlight the address with your mouse, press Ctrl-C, or Command-C on a Mac, then place the mouse in the location bar and press Ctrl-V, or Command-V on a Mac, to paste it in. Then hit <enter>.)

To move to other pages in the Web site, click on highlighted words, or, whenever your mouse cursor changes into a hand when it's positioned on an object, right-click your mouse to go there.

WHERE ARE THESE WEB PAGES LOCATED?

When you tap into the Web page of a quilter in Australia or Great Britain, yes, you really are connecting electronically to these foreign countries. It's just like calling another country long-distance. The pages themselves are physically located on the Internet service of their owner, or whatever computer is serving as the network server in that locale.

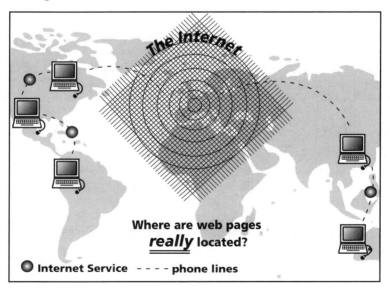

Where are web pages *really* located?

● **Internet Service** - - - - **phone lines**

URLs point you to directories on a remote computer just like directory paths (c:\windows\programs) get you to different directories and subdirectories on your computer's hard disk.

If a Web address doesn't get you to what you want, try working back through the URL. For instance, the Patchwords Web site offers a wreath pattern for machine quilting at:

http://www.patchwords.com/QPatterns/wreath.html

But if it's not there when you get there, try:

http://www.patchwords.com/QPatterns/

Or:

http://www.patchwords.com/

◆ COMMON ERROR MESSAGES WHEN YOU ENTER A WEB ADDRESS

❂ 404 NOT FOUND
The requested URL /blocks/tips.html was not found on this server.

Reason: Your browser was able to find the Internet service or the computer on which the Web site was or is hosted, but no such page was found on the service. (The very last word at the end of a URL is the page's address. For example, tips.html.) Maybe the Web site owner removed that particular page. Or perhaps the Web site no longer exists.

Fix: Try working back through the URL as explained in the above tip, to see if you can locate the Web site, or determine if the site itself is gone from the service. Also, try suffixing the page's address with "htm" or "html" instead of its current extension. For example, in place of tips.html type tips.htm. (An HTML suffix is the same as an HTM, but some Web page hosting services require that Web pages be named with one or the other. Typing the wrong extension is a common mistake.)

✋ DNS LOOKUP FAILURE or UNABLE TO LOCATE THE SERVER.

The server does not have a DNS entry.

Reason: DNS stands for "domain name server." A domain name is the first part of a URL—for instance, in www.ctpub.com, ctpub.com is the domain name. Every Internet service (and AOL) has a database of such Web page host addresses. When you type a URL, the first thing your browser does is tell your Internet service to look up the domain name in its database, to find out where it's located. If it can't find it, your Internet service's computer may poll other domain name directories around the Internet to determine if any of them know where the domain name can be found. If none of them do, you may get the error message "DNS Lookup Failure."

Why can't it find the domain name? Maybe it no longer exists. Or perhaps it's so new that the domain name databases your Internet service uses can't find it. Sometimes you also get this error message when there's heavy traffic on the Internet. Your Internet service is taking too long to look up the name, so your browser errors out.

Fix: Try typing the URL into your browser later in the day. If you still get the error message, try the URL a few days, or even a week later. If you still get error messages the domain name no longer exists.

✋ NO RESPONSE FROM SERVER

Reason: Your browser is unable to get a timely response from the Web site's host computer. This can because of heavy traffic on the Internet, or on the branch of the Internet you are traveling. It can be because the computer that's hosting the Web site is overloaded (everyone is tapping in). Or it can be because your Internet service is overloaded, or its own computers are experiencing slowdowns for technical reasons.

Fix: Try the URL either in a few minutes, or later in the day.

◆ HOW TO FIND QUILT BLOCKS, PATTERNS, RECIPES, AND MORE!

Late one night, Judy saw an ad on TV for a mouth-watering confection called "Kentucky bourbon brownie bottom pie." Mmm! Wouldn't a recipe for that be nice? she thought. She headed to one of the big Internet searchers, typed "kentucky bourbon brownie bottom pie" and within seconds had seven different recipes for it.

So forget those ten-pound Internet directories. All you need to quickly find what you want on the Internet is to head to one of these big searchers:

EXCITE www.excite.com

HOTBOT www.hotbot.com

ALTAVISTA www.digital.altavista.com

Type the name of a quilt block or pattern—or a recipe, Bible quote, or that rare disease that afflicts your Aunt Mildred—and the searcher will come up with a list of possibly applicable Web sites. Usually you can find at least one information-chocked Web site within the first two "pages" of matches. From that page you can scuttle around the Web to related links and Web pages.

Internet Explorer comes with the latest versions of America Online's software, but you can use Netscape's Navigator instead if you prefer (and many people do). Here's how: dial up AOL and make the connection. Minimize America Online's software. Fire up Navigator. Type the Web address you want to head to and you're there.

◆ HOW TO PRINT WEB PAGES, OR SELECTIONS FROM PAGES

You can print entire Web pages just like you'd print any other document on your computer screen.

First, wait until the page is transmitted completely to your computer. In Navigator you'll see what looks like snow falling through the big 'N' logo in the top right-hand corner of the screen. If you're using a Mac you'll see shooting stars. That means the page is being transmitted to your computer. In Explorer, the 'e' logo in the top right-hand corner spins as the page is downloading.

To print in Navigator, pull down the File menu and select Print Preview. Once you click the Print button in the Preview window, you'll get a dialog box in which you can choose which pages of the currently viewed Web page you wish to print. On a Macintosh, pull down the File menu and select Print.

In Internet Explorer, pull down the File menu and select Print.

On more complex Web sites your browser might ask you to specify which frame you'd like to print. A frame is a division of the page (a page with multiple frames is usually framed by multiple scroll bars, like those pictured in the Jinny Beyer Web page below). You will need to go back to the page and mouse-click the side or section you wish to print, then head back to the printing menu to print it.

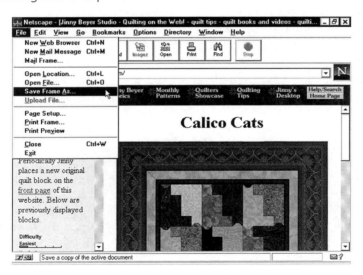

Jinny Beyer's Web site has frames—divisions that you can click between and scroll individually. In order to print the pattern on a framed page you must first click on the side of the page you wish to print in order to select it, then select Print or Print Preview from the File menu.

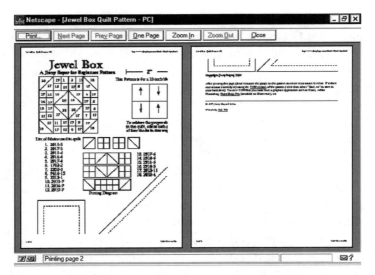

In Navigator you can preview how a Web page will look when printed. Click the Print button to send it to the printer.

✊ **BUG WARNING!** If you get nothing but blank pages when you select Print Preview in Navigator in Windows, or if nothing prints—you may have stumbled on a lingering—and terribly annoying bug found in several versions of the program. First, click on the Zoom In feature to see if the page displays as a closer view. If it does, you'll be able to print it. If nothing appears, close the print window, highlight and copy to the clipboard the URL (Ctrl-C) and close down the browser. Reload Navigator, past the URL into the Address bar, and press <enter>. With any luck the page will print on your second try. Another trick is to select the entire page then issue the print command.

Remember, Web Pages Are Copyrighted! Web pages are copyrighted just as any publication is. Or any quilt design, for that matter. You should not print them, except for your own personal use, without asking permission from the Web page's owner. The same holds true for any elements on the page, including text, but also graphics. Never, ever print or distribute these things—or, heaven forbid, put them on your own Web page—or use them in your quilt without permission.

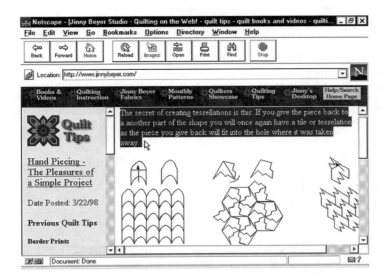

You can also print sections of a Web page by highlighting with your mouse the sections you wish to print, copying it into the clipboard, pasting it into your word processor and printing it there. This page shows one of Jinny Beyer's monthly tips—this example is on creating tessellations.

◆ HOW TO SAVE WEB PAGES TO YOUR COMPUTER'S DISK

You can save entire Web pages to your disk so that you can peruse them later, but keep in mind the above warning—these pages are copyrighted and you should not distribute them.

First the page must be completely loaded.

Remember to click on the frame you wish to save.

In your browser, from the File menu select Save as... A pop-up box will give you a choice of saving the page as HTML or text (shown on page 19). If you're using a Mac, the pop-up box will give you the option of saving the text as source, which is the same as HTML.

HTML is the coding that is used to format Web pages—it's similar to text, but with a few weird notations thrown in. Save the page in HTML format if you plan to view it later with your browser while you're off-line. (To view it in your browser later, from the File menu select Open Page. On a Mac, select Open Page in Navigator. Click Choose File, then click your way to the file stored on your hard disk. Once you've found it, click the Open button.)

If you want to merely pull up the Web page's text in your word processor, and perhaps print it later, save it as Text.

Neither of these features will let you save the page's images, however. To save the graphics you need to:

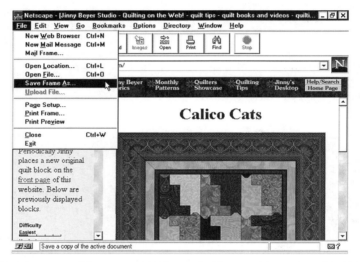

Your browser will let you save Web pages either as plain text or with their HTML formatting, but neither option will save graphics. You'll need to save each image individually.

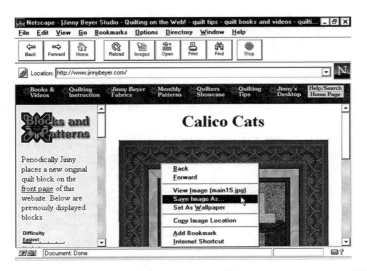

In order to save a picture off the Web, right-click on it in Windows or click-hold on a Mac and select Save Image As... . Remember though that these images are copyrighted by their artist and you should not print or distribute them without asking permission first.

◆ HOW TO CAPTURE IMAGES YOU FIND ON THE INTERNET

Images on Web pages are copyrighted just like text is. If you want to use them in any way—either to print to distribute to your quilt guild or post on your own Web pages—the same rules apply as to text: you need to ask the owner's permission first!

Position your cursor over the image and right-click. On a Mac click-hold. A menu box will pop up. Select Save Image As... or Save Picture As... . You can later view it in either your browser or a graphics program like Paint Shop Pro. You can even import it into a word processing document. (In Microsoft Word, from the Insert menu select Picture.)

◆ HOW TO DOWNLOAD SOFTWARE FROM THE INTERNET

In most instances all you need to do is mouse-click on the highlighted name of the program or file on a Web page and your browser will start downloading—hopefully by prompting you where you want to store the file (shown below).

But sometimes that doesn't work. If that happens, right-click in Windows or click-hold on a Mac on the name of the file. When a pop-up menu appears, click on Save Link As... and the browser will begin downloading.

The Quilt-Pro Systems Web site (http://www. quiltpro.com) *offers demos of its quilt design software that you can download for free.*

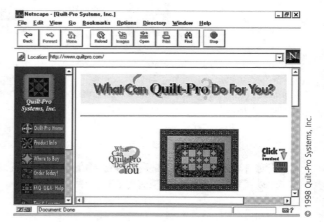

In most instances all you need to do is click on a highlighted program or file name in order to download it.

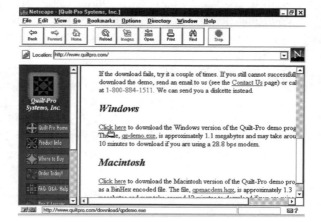

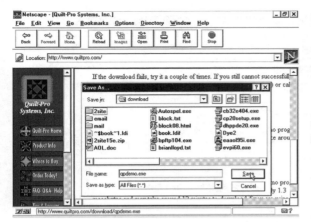

Once you click on the file name your browser will ask you where on your computer you want to store the software. Once you select a directory, click Save.

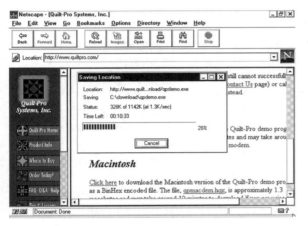

Once the file begins transferring, this box will pop up, showing you the progress of the download.

Should the file transfer progress box (shown above) disappear, don't panic. Its disappearance does not mean your computer has stopped downloading the file. For instance, sometimes it disappears if you click on something else on the Web page or in your browser. You will probably find the transfer box tucked away in some other corner of your computer screen (like the bottom program status bar) and the transfer still faithfully chugging away in the background.

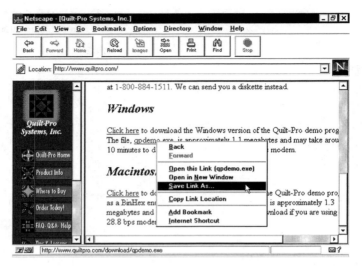

Say you can't get your browser to download software in a sane fashion. Maybe it spits kooky characters across the screen when you try. (This is what happens to Judy, who's installed on her computer so many ill-advised software doodads she's found on the Internet, that nothing on her computer works in a normal fashion.) There's a simple way out: right-click in Windows or click-hold on a Mac on the file name so the above menu box pops up. Select Save Link As... and you'll be on your way.

One thing to keep in mind is that if the file transfer progress box flashes on your screen, then disappears, your browser may not have saved the file. That will be because it's not tapped into the correct Web page to actually download the file. You should be on the Web page that displays the highlighted file name, or a "Download now" link. In other words, you need to be exactly one mouse click away from the file download in order to get this to work.

As a file download starts, always check that the file is writing itself to your disk with the same name as it's stored on the remote computer, so you know what it is and where to find it.

❓ WHAT DO YOU DO WITH SOFTWARE ONCE YOU DOWNLOAD IT, or WHAT DOES THAT ZIP OR SIT AT THE END OF ITS NAME MEAN?

When you download software from a Web site it's usually compressed. That means that the file has been shrunk so that it takes less time to transfer to your computer.

PKZIP by PKWare (**http://www.pkware.com**) is the most commonly used compression format in the PC world. When a file has a .ZIP extension it has been compressed with PKZIP. You'll need to download PKZIP in order to uncompress it.

Stuffit by Aladdin Sofware (**http://www.aladdinsys.com**) is the compression program used with Macintoshes. Software compressed with Stuffit ends with .SIT, and you'll need to download Stuffit in order to expand it.

What about files ending with .EXE? They're self-extracting, which means that you merely click on them in order to uncompress them.

HOW TO SEND E-MAIL

If you're using America Online all you need to do is click on the You Have Mail icon on the greeting screen to read your e-mail or send mail, even out on the Internet. (To send messages to someone on the Internet from AOL, type the full Internet address—for example ctinfo@ctpub.com—into the To: line in the AOL mail screen just as you'd type an AOL address.)

If you're using an Internet service you can use special mail software like Eudora or Pegasus. Or, you can use the mail program built into your browser.

In Navigator, press Ctrl-2 to get to the mail box (shown on page 24). On a Mac, click the Mail icon box in the lower right-hand corner of the brower's screen to get to your in-box. Command-T retrieves new e-mail.

In Explorer, click the Mail icon in the upper right-hand corner of the browser's screen to load the Outlook Express mail program.

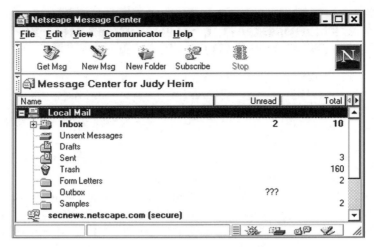

Press Ctrl-2 in Windows to get to your mail in Navigator.

 ## YOU WILL NEED TO SET UP YOUR BROWSER'S MAIL PROGRAM IN ORDER TO SEND MAIL.

In order for your browser to send and retrieve mail through your ISP for the first time, you'll need to tell it the name of your ISP's computer where it stores mail. You can probably guess the name of this computer. It's probably named "mail." For instance, if your e-mail address is sue@biginternet.com, Big Internet's mail computer is probably named mail.biginternet.com.

Or, maybe not. Regardless, your Internet service should tell you the name of the computer where it stores mail so you can enter this vital information into your mail program. Your Internet e-mail address and password are essentially all the browser needs to know to be able to send and receive mail.

 ## SETTING UP NAVIGATOR

From Navigator's Edit menu select Preferences. Under the Mail & Groups category, select Mail Server. Type in your user name on the ISP, and the names of the incoming and outgoing mail servers. Click OK when you're finished.

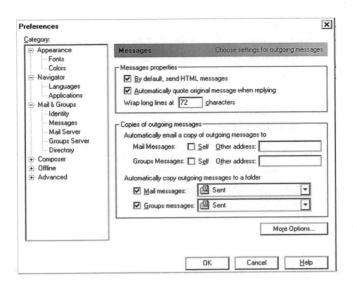

You can set up Navigator to send and retrieve mail through your ISP by heading to this setup box. Get to it by selecting Preferences from the Edit menu, then scrolling through the setup menu list on the left.

▶ SETTING UP EXPLORER

In Explorer's Outlook Express, from the Tools menu select Accounts. Click the Add button and select Mail to start the wizard that will guide you through the mail set-up process. When you're done you should have settings like those shown below.

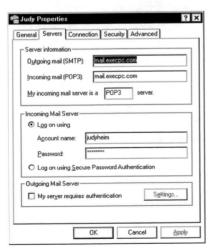

When Outlook Express is set up successfully to send and retrieve mail you should have a settings box similar to this (you can reach it by pulling down the Tools menu and selecting Accounts. Head to the Mail tab, highlight the account name, and click the Properties button).

Judy's e-mail address is judyheim@execpc.com, so notice that her outgoing SMTP mail server is named—you guessed it, mail.execpc.com. Even if your ISP gave you erroneous directions for setting up your mail program, you can make a few simple deductions from your e-mail address to fill in the blanks.

SENDING AND RECEIVING MAIL WITH NAVIGATOR

Press Ctrl-2 to get to Navigator's mail program. On a Mac, click the Mail icon box in the lower right-hand corner of the brower's screen. To download your mail from your Internet service, click the Get Msg icon, then type your ISP password when prompted.

To send a message, click the New Msg icon. After you're finished writing, click the Send icon to dial your ISP and send it immediately. Or pull down the File menu and select Send Later for Navigator to store it in its outbox.

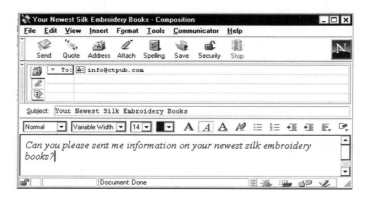

You can write your message in different fonts and colors with Navigator's mail program. You can even add pictures by heading to the Insert menu and selecting Image. But your recipient won't be able to see the special effects unless they're using another HTML-compatible mail program like that in Explorer.

SENDING AND RECEIVING MAIL WITH EXPLORER

Head to Outlook Express by clicking the Mail icon in Explorer's right-hand corner. Press Ctrl-N or Command-N on a Mac to pop up a message composition form. When you're done writing, click the Send button. Take note that this will only store it in Outlook's outbox. To actually send it you need to click the Send and Receive button on the top of Outlook's main screen so that the program dials your Internet service and checks and sends mail.

Can you (or should you) send e-mail messages festooned with pictures and color? The mail programs found in the latest versions of Explorer and Navigator are what's called HTML or rich text compatible. That means you can use them to send—and read—mail with the same kind of formatting found on Web pages. And the same sorts of pictures too—like GIF and JPG images.

America Online can also send and read some HTML coding in messages, but not all.

Should you bedeck your e-mail with pictures of quilt blocks and fancy signatures? Probably not.

First, graphics take much longer than text to download. And no one likes to sit twiddling their fingers as their mail program chugs to capture some humongous e-mail message they were not expecting.

Second, many people use text-only e-mail programs like Eudora that will display that rich text as gibberish.

Maybe this will change someday. Maybe everyone will have super-fast links into the Internet and HTML-friendly e-mail programs. Until then, write your messages in old-fashioned plain text. (That means avoiding Explorer's "stationary" feature, and turning off the rich text setting. You can find it by pulling down the Tools menu and selecting Options. Under the Send tab, check Plain Text, then click the Apply button.)

◆ HOW TO TALK TO OTHER QUILTERS ON THE INTERNET

There are several ways besides e-mail in which you can talk to quilters around the world via the Internet:

◐ *Message Boards on Web Sites* —

Many quilting Web sites offer message or bulletin boards where you can post and read messages on topics ranging from batting brands to piecing techniques. Often these discussions are lively and informative, because they're so easy to tap into and they remain on the Web site for so long. All you need to do to join in is to type the URL into your browser.

◐ *Usenet Newsgroups* —

Newsgroups are public messages that swirl through the Internet in bulletin board style. To tap in you'd use the news feature of your browser, or special news reading software. There is only one discussion group devoted to quilting, although several focus on general needlework topics. While Usenet's quilting discussion group is worthwhile, you'll find better quilting discussions in mailing lists.

◐ *Mailing Lists* —

Dozens of mailing lists are devoted to quilting, many focusing on special topics like using Electric Quilt or working as a quilt teacher. Mailing lists are where you'll find the best quilt discussions on the Internet. (Mailing lists are also where you find the most worthwhile information on the Internet on just about any topic.)

You don't tap into a Web site to participate. You send an e-mail message to a computer (or person) to subscribe to the list. Each day e-mail from other quilters on the mailing list finds its way to your mailbox. To participate in the discussion you send your message to a central computer that broadcasts it to everyone on the list. Some quilt mailing lists have as many as a thousand subscribers. You can find a guide to quilt-related mailing lists on Sue Traudt's World-Wide Quilting Web page (**http://quilt.com/MainQuiltingPage.html**).

Online Service Quilt Discussion Forums —

All the major online services, including America Online, CompuServe, and Microsoft Network, offer lively quilt discussion forums, where you can palaver with other quilters, view quilts, and download software and patterns. To get to them, use the service's keyword or "go" word feature, and type quilting.

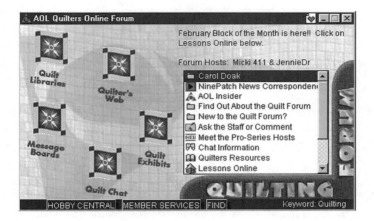

America Online hosts a terrific quilting forum, with message boards, software and pattern libraries, and 24-hour chat. To get there, use the keyword quilting (Ctrl-K, or Command-K on a Mac).

Chat Rooms —

Aren't chat rooms those notorious dens where lascivious strangers type to each other at 2 a.m.? Yes, but there are also chat rooms for quilters. Quilters aren't as avid chatters as, say, Dungeons & Dragons fans, but they do enjoy logging on to chat occasionally. AOL has a quilt chat room (shown on the next page). CompuServe also offers some chatting facilities in its quilting forum—use the go word quilting to get there. You can also find chatting—scheduled as well as impromptu—on various quilting Web sites. You'll need to download and run special chat software to join in. The pages include directions. The most famous is the #QuiltChat site (**http://www.kathkwilts.com**) by Kathy Sommers.

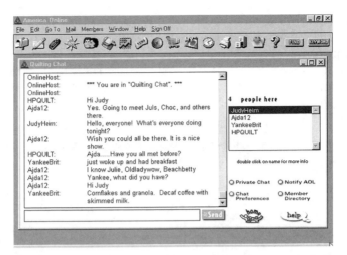

Feeling lonely at 3 a.m. on a weekday night? Jump into the quilt chat on America Online. To get there press Ctrl-K, or Command-K on a Mac, and type quilting <enter>. Then click on the #QuiltChat icon.

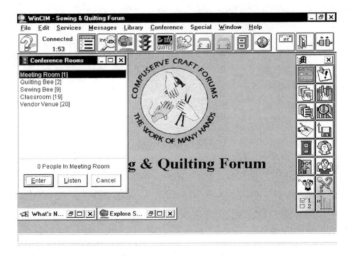

CompuServe's quilting forum offers chat as well as messaging features. To join in head to the forum by using the go word (click the green light icon) quilting. Once you're in the forum, click on the door icon on the right side of your screen to find out who's chatting.

◆ HOW TO READ USENET NEWSGROUPS WITH YOUR WEB BROWSER

Participating in Web site message boards or mailing lists is fairly straightforward, so long as you know how to use your Web browser and mail program. But setting up your browser to read newsgroups can be tricky. The first time you want to read a newsgroup you'll need to download from your Internet service a list of current newsgroups. Then you'll need to search it and subscribe to the groups you're interested in. Finally, you need to download the messages themselves. Here's how to do it with Navigator and Explorer:

HOW TO READ THE USENET QUILTING NEWSGROUP WITH NAVIGATOR

1. You must first set up your browser to retrieve newsgroups from your Internet server. Find out from your Internet server the name of the computer where newsgroups are stored. (It will be something like groups.myisp.com.) Pull down the Edit menu and select Preferences. Under Mail & Groups, head to the Group Server setup box (shown on next page) and enter your ISP information. Click OK to save it.

2. Connect to your Internet service.

3. Head to Navigator's message center by pressing Ctrl-2 or click the Mail icon box in the lower right-hand corner of the brower's screen on a Mac.

4. From the File menu, select Subscribe to Discussion Groups.

5. Click the All Groups tab to download a list of current newsgroups. This may take a while since the list is large. The message "Receiving discussion groups" should appear on the very bottom line of the screen (shown top of page 33).

6. When that humongous list of newsgroups has finished downloading, head to the Search for a Group tab. Type "quilt" in the search box (or whatever you're interested in) and click the Search Now button. Type "textiles" instead to get a full list of all the needlecraft-related newsgroups.

7. Once the newsgroup searcher has come up with a list of interesting newsgroups, highlight the one you want to read (shown middle of next page), and press the Subscribe button. A check will appear beside it.

8. To read your newsgroup, head back to the message center (Ctrl-2 or click the Mail icon box on a Mac). From the pull-down menu box at the top of the screen, select the newsgroup (rec.crafts.textiles.quilting) and click Download Messages. You may want to download only a selection (under 500 for example) and mark as read the rest of the messages. This way, the next time you download messages from the newsgroup, you will only download the newest ones.

9. From the Go menu you can move from thread to thread, reading messages and skipping others.

10. In the future to read messages, go to the message center (Ctrl-2 or click the Mail icon box on a Mac). From the pull-down menu box at the top of the screen, select the newsgroup (rec.crafts.textiles.quilting) you want to read. From the File menu select Get Messages/New.

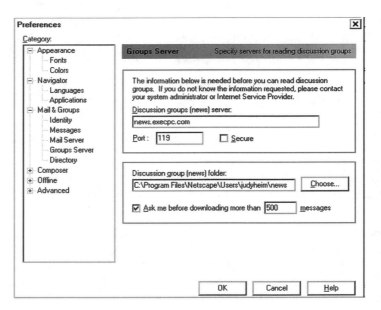

First you need to tell Navigator the name of the server on your ISP where newsgroups are stored.

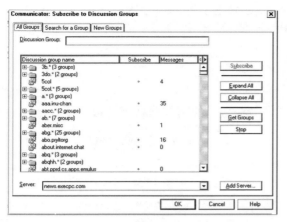

You need to download the complete list of newsgroups in order to search for the needlework ones.

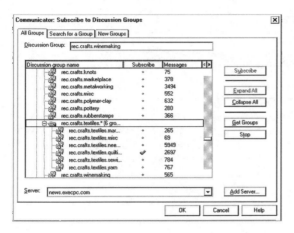

After you download and search the newsgroups, subscribe to the groups you want to read by selecting them.

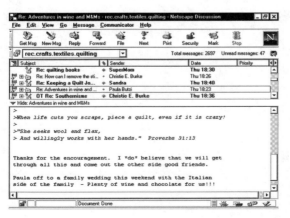

Select the messages and message threads you want to read and they'll appear in the bottom of the screen. (If you don't get a split screen you may need to "pull up" the bottom portion of the screen with your mouse. In other words, the window is there, it's just hidden.)

HOW TO READ THE USENET QUILTING NEWSGROUP WITH EXPLORER

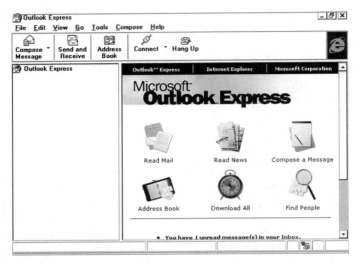

1. Load the Outlook Express mail portion of Internet Explorer by clicking on the mailbox icon on the top right-hand corner of the screen. Click the Read News icon on the Express screen. If you have not yet set it up to read newsgroups with your ISP, a setup wizard will appear. It will prompt you for your name, e-mail address, and the name of the dial-up connection you use to connect to your ISP. Most important of all it will ask you the name of the server on your ISP where the news messages can be found.

2. The next time you click Express's Read News icon it will ask you if you'd like to download a list of the newsgroups from your ISP. This may take a while since there are tens of thousands of newsgroups.

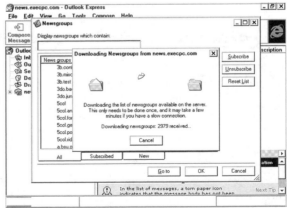

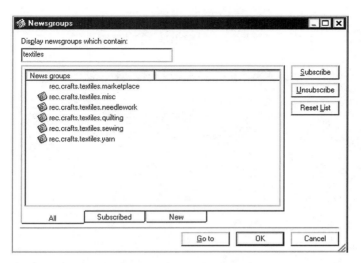

3. Type "textiles" to search the list for newsgroups that contain "textiles" in their name—and to get a full list of the needlework-related newsgroups. Subscribe to them by highlighting each, clicking the Subscribe button. Then click OK when you're done.

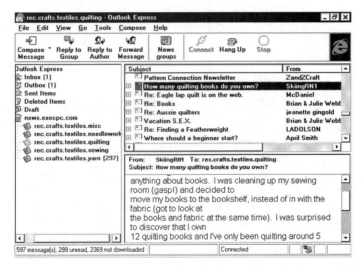

4. To read newsgroups that you've subscribed to, click on the name of the newsgroup on the left side of the screen. To read individual messages, click on the headers displayed at the top right of the screen.

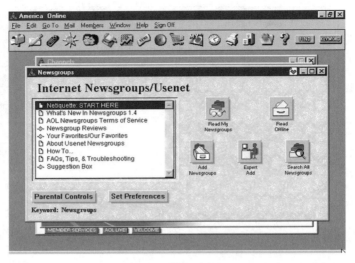

HOW TO READ THE USENET QUILTING NEWSGROUP ON AMERICA ONLINE

1. To read the Internet newsgroups through AOL press Ctrl-K, or Command-K on a Mac, and type the keyword newsgroups. Click on the Search Newsgroups icon to search the tens of thousands of newsgroups for ones in your interests. (Some search words that work are: quilting, textiles, cross-stitch, sewing, knitting, weaving.)

2. Once you click the Search Newsgroups icon, type your search word and click Search.

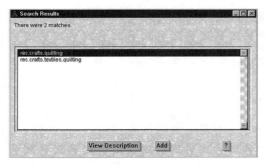

3. Once AOL comes up with a list of matching newsgroups, click the Add button to add selected newsgroups to the list of newsgroups that you wish to read.

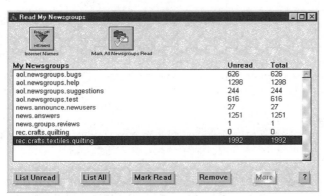

4. Head back to the main newsgroup menu by closing the windows (click the X in the upper right-hand corner). Click the Read My Newsgroups button to pop up a list of the newsgroups to which you're subscribed. Click the List Unread button to list messages in the newsgroups that you have not yet read.

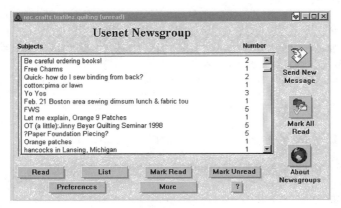

5. To read listed messages and their replies, highlight the message and click the Read button.

❷ HOW SAFE IS THE INTERNET?

Everytime Judy's mom hears that her daughter's been surfing the Web, she gasps, "Be careful! That Internet is not safe!"

The Internet is safer than the average subway station—but sometimes not by much. We know you're an adult and will take care of yourself just as you would in a subway station. But just so you know we're concerned about your safety, just like Judy's mother is of her daughter's, here are the major Judy-and-Gloria warnings:

✋ **Never give anyone your credit card number, any of your online passwords, or any personal information such as your street address or phone number.**

An all-too-common ruse is for hackers to e-mail a new subscriber to America Online alleging they are a representative of AOL and need the subscriber to resubmit their credit card number for verification. Hackers sent Gloria instant messages requesting her password. (She copied and pasted the messages into an e-mail which she sent to AOL management at the complaint box at TOSspam.)

✋ **Beware of get-rich-quick offers that arrive by the mega-byte in your e-mail box. And never answer junk e-mail.**

You'll either be bombarded with more e-mail, or the sender may retaliate if you ask to be removed from their mailing list. (That happened to a prominent woman in the craft industry. An angry junk e-mailer mail-bombed her company's e-mail server after she asked to be removed from his mailing list.)

✋ **If you shop on the Web, pay with a credit card in case there are problems. Never type your credit card into any Web site that's not a "secure" Web site.**

Secure means that the site will encrypt the information you send it. As you enter a secure site your browser will tell you that it's secure. Also, Navigator will display a lock icon.

✋ **Be sure to supervise your children on the Net.**

The best way is to talk to them regularly about what they're doing online. Warn them as often as you can not to meet in person a stranger they may meet online, even if they insist the new friend is another child—sometimes they're not.

❓ WILL MY COMPUTER CATCH A VIRUS?

Viruses are noxious bits of program code that travel in computer files—usually program files—and plant themselves on your disk for the purpose of wreaking havoc.

The best way to avoid contracting a virus is to scan with a virus-checker any program that you download from the Internet, prior to running it. Our favorite is the $50 Norton AntiVirus from Symantec (**http://www.symantec.com**, 800/441-7234, 541/334-6054). One of the best things about this program is that regular updates to its virus database are free. (Be sure to keep that database updated once you install the program!)

You should also scan any disk of software that you buy, or CD-ROM, prior to installing it. Several viruses have been spread through commercially distributed software.

You should be especially careful to scan any disks that have been in your work computer, or come from the computers of your child's friends.

You should not open any file attachment that comes with an e-mail message from a stranger. Delete it, and if it was ever dangerous, your computer will never know.

Your computer cannot contract a virus by your tapping into a Web site or reading an e-mail message. Passing disks between work, school, and home computers is the most common way in which viruses are spread.

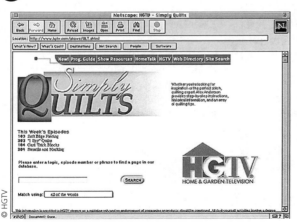

The cable channel Home & Garden Television hosts quilting and craft discussions that anyone can join at **http://www.hgtv.com.**

free Big Quilting Web Sites

If you're just getting started on the Web, where should you go first? The quilting Web sites in this chapter, we think. They have everything: free patterns, lots of tips, monthly block and fabric swaps, good conversation, and lots of friendly quilters. In the beginning of this book we warn that Web sites come and go and it is unavoidable that some of the addresses may be gone by the time you look for them. However, the Web sites in this chapter have been around so long they're institutions. Bookmark them in your browser, and know they'll be there when you need them.

All these sites also offer lots of hotlinks to all the newest and neatest quilting stuff on the Internet. Consider them portals into the quilting world in cyberspace. While you're visiting be sure to drop a note of gratitude to the site's "webmistress" or "master." The quilters who run these mega-sites do so for little or no compensation—and running sites like this can be a full-time job.

DELPHI QUILTING FORUM
http://www.delphi.com/quilting

DELPHI SEWING FORUM
http://www.delphi.com/needle

DELPHI TEXTILE ARTS FORUM
http://www.delphi.com/textile

One of the first commercial online services ever was a quirky (but cheap) service known as Delphi. It attracted a carefree, if intense, group of quilters, sewers, spinners, and knitters. Delphi's conversation forums are now available for free through the Web. They've blossomed into incredible resources with files, conversations, magazine-like features—and lots of knowledgeable people everywhere. The quilting and sewing forums are run by Judy Smith, the textile one by Rita Levine. You can tap into them through their Web pages, and they're all worth checking out.

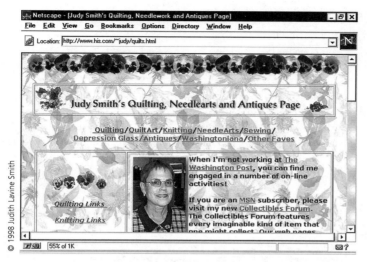

*Judy Smith's Web site (**http://www.his.com/~judy/quilts.html**) is another one you can rely on as a portal into the cyber-quilting world. Judy runs a number of great online forums.*

DOWN UNDER QUILTS
http://www.duquilts.com.au/

Down Under Quilts is an Australian quilting magazine. Its Web site offers information, links, patterns, and news that quilters on any continent will find valuable.

NATIONAL ONLINE QUILTERS
http://www.noqers.org

Cheryl Simmerman (a.k.a. "Loons") runs this beehive of quilters who've been together for years. You'll love the chatter and the swaps. The news and features are as good as in any quilting magazine.

PLANET PATCHWORK
http://www.planetpatchwork.com

Rob Holland's Planet is the home to his e-zine Virtual Quilter, page 151 (also see Chapter 16, Free Quilt Magazines, for more information on Web-based quilting magazines). But Rob offers lots of other good stuff, like exhaustive links to all the quilting goodies on the Web.

QUILTART
http://www.quiltart.com

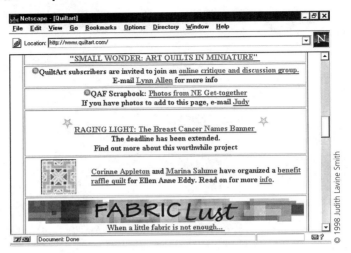

You can always count on the QuiltArt site for lots of news, chatter, and goings-on.

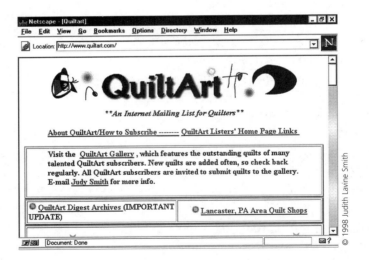

QuiltArt is a mailing list devoted to discussing quilts that are beyond traditional (look to Chapter 15, Free Online Quilt Discussions, for more information on how to tap into mailing lists). But its Web site, run by Judy Smith, offers loads of information, news, and chatter for quilters of all persuasions.

QUILTBEE
http://needlearts.dm.net/quiltbee/

The QuiltBee site is devoted to the mailing list of the same name. Among the activities of this 800+ member quilting sorority: a birthday club, "secret angels," mystery quilts, and fabric and block swaps galore. This site also offers a nice directory of links to other quilting sites on the Web.

#QUILTCHAT
http://kathkwilts.com/

QuiltChat is an Internet "chat" channel for quilters, but you don't need to participate in chats to find friends and information at this huge Web site for quilters, run by Kathy Somers.

QUILTER'S ONLINE RESOURCE
http://www.nmia.com/~mgdesign/qor/index.html

Mary Graham runs this site, which is full of patterns, projects, news, tips, and chatter.

QUILTING AT THE MINING CO.
http://quilting.miningco.com/

You'll find lots of good stuff at the Mining Co., from great feature articles to free patterns and links to other quilt-related information on the Web. Susan Druding of San Francisco's Straw Into Gold

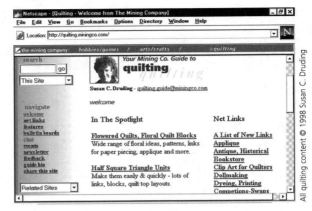

*is the quilting "guide" at this preeminent leisure-interest Web site. You'll find Susan's weekly articles, plus links, patterns, tips, and much more. There's even a bulletin board and chat feature. While you're at The Mining Co., check out its other special interest pages like Sewing (***http://sewing. miningco. com/***) and Arts & Crafts Business (***http://artsandcrafts. miningco.com/ index.htm***). To find portions of this sometimes-hard-to-navigate Web site devoted to your other needlecraft interests head to its hobby index page (***http://home.miningco.com/hobbies/***).*

SUE TRAUDT'S WORLD WIDE QUILTING PAGE
http://quilt.com/MainQuiltingPage.html

The Mother of All Quilting Web Sites: It's Sue Traudt's World Wide Quilting site. It's like a cyber-city devoted to quilting. Sue's was the first quilting page on the Web, and it continues to be the best. Sue has everything on

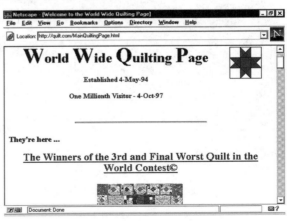

this site: frequently-asked question files from quilting mailing lists; links to just about everything the Internet offers quilters; plus lots and lots of free patterns and advice.

BOOKMARK YOUR FAVORITE WEB SITES
http://www.keepsake.com

Pull down the drop-down history list in your browser to quickly click your way back to Web sites you've previously visited.

It's easy to get lost on the Web, and sometimes difficult to find your way back to a great Web site you may have visited a half hour ago—or yesterday. You can find Web sites you've previously visited by pulling down the history list in the top bar of your browser. But your browser records in that history list only URLs that you've actually typed into its location bar; in other words, it won't record URLs that you've clicked your way through to Web links.

The solution is to bookmark favorite sites. To do so all you need to do is click the Bookmark button on your Web browser, or pull down the bookmark menu and select Add Bookmark. In Internet Explorer pull down the Favorites menu and click Add to Favorites.

CHAPTER 3

free Quilt Patterns

What quilter doesn't want every quilt pattern in the universe? Click your way around the Internet and you'll have them soon enough. Oodles of free quilt patterns, from traditional pieced to holiday appliqué, float through cyberspace. Some are products of quilt magazines and publishers, others have been drawn by famous designers and by lesser-known, talented quilters like you and me.

Just remember that if you print these patterns to give to friends, always include the name and Web site address of the designer and any applicable copyright notices. Most of these patterns are provided for "personal use" only. If you want to hand them out free at a store or quilt guild meeting, always ask the owner for permission first. The owners of many of these Web sites change their patterns regularly, so be sure to drop in frequently.

And remember: whenever you print or save to disk a quilt pattern, always drop an e-mail of thanks to the Web site owner. Note: We've included the main URL of the Web sites below, along with the URL of the specific page where patterns can be found. If the pattern page URL doesn't work, try the main URL. Web site owners often change the URLs of their pattern pages.

If, while working backwards through the URL, you get "access denied" messages, don't be deterred. That's the remote computer's way of telling you that there's a computer directory there, but you can't access its contents without typing a specific page name. Keep working backward through the address until you find something.

ADAPTATIONS OF 1995 G STREET FABRICS BLOCK-OF-THE-MONTH CONTEST
http://www.his.com/~queenb/flowers.html

BENARTEX QUILT FABRICS
http://www.benartex.com/

Quilt fabric-maker Benartex offers free quilt patterns to promote its fabric lines.

THE CANADIAN QUILTER'S ASSOCIATION
http://members.tripod.com/~cqaacc/
http://members.tripod.com/~cqaacc/patterns.htm

You'll find patterns for a quilter's tote bag and a baby quilt.

CANADIAN QUILTERS ONLINE
http://www.barint.on.ca/~wfitzger/pp-leaf.html

A free paper-pieced pattern for a Maple Leaf block—are you surprised?

CHRISTMAS ORNAMENT FOUNDATION PIECED PATTERNS
http://www.nmia.com/~mgdesign/qor/ornament.htm

DAVID SMALL'S SMALL EXPRESSIONS
http://www.ici.net/~quilters

Small Expressions offers a new free foundation block pattern each month.

DAWN DUPERAULT'S WEB SITE
http://ares.redsword.com/dduperault

- *Cathedral Windows Quilt Pattern*
  http://ares.redsword.com/dduperault/circle.htm

  This one includes lots of delicate handiwork.

- *Quillow Pattern*
  http://ares.redsword.com/dduperault/quillow.htm

  A "quillow" is a cross between a pillow and quilt. It originated Down Under, just like a koala.

DEANNA SPINGOLA'S WATERCOLOR MAGIC
http://www.spingola.com/ds

A new block pattern each month from Deanna's collection.

DEBBY KRATOVIL'S A QUILTER BY DESIGN
http://www.his.com/~queenb/

DELPHI'S QUILTING ART
http://www.delphi.com/quilting/

A free block of the month.

FOUNDATION-PIECED CHRISTMAS TREE WALL-HANGING PATTERN
http://www.nmia.com/~mgdesign/qor/xmastree.htm

JC QUILTS
http://home.earthlink.net/~jwestergren/

Free patterns-of-the-month that include pieced and foundation-pieced blocks, plus lots of tips.

When you tap into a pattern page don't forget to wait until the full page loads ("Document done" will flash on the bottom of your browser), then use the scroll bars to scroll down to see the full page.

JINNY BEYER STUDIOS
http://www.jinnybeyer.com

You'll love this site! Each month Jinny posts a new pattern from her drawing table.

JOEN WOLFROM'S WEB SITE
http://www.mplx.com/joenwolfrom/index.html
http://www.mplx.com/joenwolfrom/monthly.htm

Artist and author Joen Wolfrom offers free patterns each month. She also includes recipes like crab dip!

LAURIE'S GOOD LIVING BLOCK LIBRARY
http://www.brookdale.cc.nj.us/staff/pac/lbender/index.html
http://www.brookdale.cc.nj.us/staff/pac/lbender/quilting.html

A large library of quilt blocks and tips from Laurie Bender.

LISA WASHBURN'S TEXAS QUILTING PAGE
http://home.sprynet.com/sprynet/mrmago01/quilting.htm

Lisa offers a new paper-pieced foundation pattern each month.

MARY GRAHAM DESIGNS
http://www.nmia.com/~mgdesign/
http://www.nmia.com/~mgdesign/qor/ufo.htm

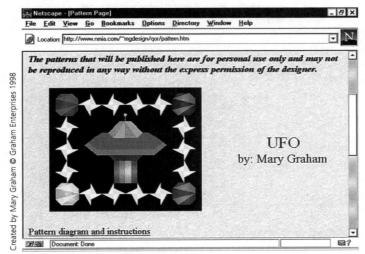

*You can get this wonderful spaceship pattern from Mary Graham Designs'
Web site. We bet you know a little child who'd love a quilt like this.*

PAPER PANACHE
http://www.PAPERPANACHE.com/

*Linda Worland runs this nifty site for her pattern letter featuring
paper-pieced patterns. You'll find free samples on the site.*

PAPER PIECING PATTERN LIBRARY
http://www.his.com/~queenb/pc.patterns.html

PATCHWORK PARTNERS BIBLICAL BLOCKS
http://www.mountain-inter.net/~graham/partners.html
http://www.mountain-inter.net/~graham/partners.html

*Biblical block patterns are hard to find, but Kim offers some
good ones.*

THE PATCHWORK STUDIO BLOCK OF THE MONTH CLUB
http://www1.islandnet.com/~agreig/blkmonth.htm

Free blocks-of-the-month with directions and patterns.

PC PIECERS
http://bankswith.apollotrust.com/~larryb/PCPiecers.htm
http://bankswith.apollotrust.com/~larryb/patterns.htm

PC Piecers offers reams of foundation piecing patterns for things like a daffodil, shamrock, and a beach bum. They also offer an "inspirational lesson" on designing foundation piecing patterns.

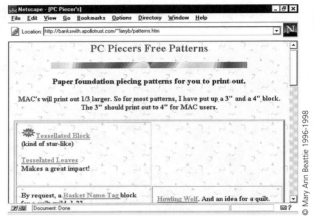

© Mary Ann Beattie 1996-1998

THE PERFECT SQUARE
http://www.webworldinc.com/perfectsquare/

Free patterns, including a block of the month. Check back regularly because patterns change.

QUILT MAGAZINE
http://www.quiltmag.com/

Quilt Magazine offers loads of free patterns. Check this site regularly because the patterns change often. Here are the addresses of its collections:

- *Free Pattern Library*
  http://www.quiltmag.com/patterns/patterns.html

- *Paper Piecing Patterns*
  http://www.quilttalk.com/paperpiece/pp.html

- *Remember Me Blocks*
  http://www.quiltmag.com/lessons/rememberme/rememberme.html

QUILTER'S HOT PACK
http://ares.redsword.com/dduperault/hotpads.htm

A pattern for a hot (or cold) pack.

SUE TRAUDT'S WIDE WORLD QUILTING
http://quilt.com

This site is so big you could get lost on it for months and not be found. Here are the addresses of the site's free pattern collections:

- *Traditional Patterns*
  http://quilt.com/QuiltBlocksPage.html

- *Foundation Patterns*
  http://quilt.com/Foundations/Foundations.html

- *Block of the Month*
  http://quilt.com/BlockOfTheMonth/BlockOfTheMonth97.html

WATERCOLOR QUILTS BY WHIMS
http://www.continet.com/whims

You'll find a free watercolor quilt pattern at this site for watercolor quilt fabrics and kits.

THE WIDE WORLD QUILTING PAGE
http://quilt.com/

Head to "Free Quilting Thread, Notions, and Tools Advice," Chapter 7 for a list of the Web sites of thread and ribbon manufacturers. Many offer free patterns and project directions.

Head to TV Show Web Sites for Project Sheets.
Many of the TV quilting and craft shows run a Web site
where you can find archives of free patterns and directions
for projects that have been featured on past shows. They
might also include information on products used in the
show, with hotlinks to the manufacturers' Web sites.
We've asterisked the sites that offer free quilt patterns.

THE CAROL DUVALL SHOW
http://www.hgtv.com/shows/CDS.shtml

*ELEANOR BURNS' QUILT-IN-A-DAY
http://www.quilt-in-a-day.com/qiad/

*Eleanor
Burns offers
free patterns
and tips
from her
show at her
Web site.*

*QUILTING FOR THE '90S, WITH KAYE WOOD
http://www.kayewood.com/

*QUILTING FROM THE HEARTLAND
http://www.qheartland.com/project.htm

*SEWING WITH NANCY, WITH NANCY ZIEMAN
http://www.nancysnotions.com/

SEW PERFECT, WITH SANDRA BETZINA
http://www3.hgtv.com/shows/SEW.shtml

SIMPLY QUILTS, WITH ALEX ANDERSON
http://www3.hgtv.com/shows/QLT.shtml

 Quilting How-Tos

Our great-grandmothers taught quilting in kitchens and parlors. Wouldn't they be surprised to learn that one day their techniques would be taught on computers and spread around the world via phone lines and something called the Internet? You can find literally thousands of quilting how-tos on the Web—directions on how to paper piece blocks, draw eight-point stars, stitch needle-turn appliqué, or get a quilt to lay flat. You'll even find advice on how to hand-quilt.

Here are some of our favorite quilting how-to Web sites. By the time you read this there will surely be many more.

 Free Piecing and Template How-tos

ALANA CONEEN SHOWS YOU HOW TO DRAFT TEMPLATES
http://www.mk.net/~coneen/quilters/how to/template.html

ALANA CONEEN SHOWS YOU HOW TO ASSEMBLE AN EIGHT-POINTED STAR
http://www.mk.net/~coneen/quilters/how to/eight/index.html

DAVID K. SMALL SHOWS YOU HOW TO DRAFT AN EIGHT-POINTED STAR
http://www.ici.net/cust_pages/quilter/text3.htm

DAVID K. SMALL SHOWS YOU HOW TO PAPER PIECE
http://www.ici.net/~quilter/howto.htm

DEBRA WEISS'S "OUTRAGEOUS FOUNDATION PIECING" FROM QUILT GALLERY MAGAZINE
http://www.quiltgallery.com/technique1.htm

ELSIE VREDENBURG SHOWS YOU HOW TO PIECE WITH FREEZER PAPER
http://users.netonecom.net/~elf/cardinal.htm

FOUNDATION PAPER-PIECING LESSON FROM #QUILTTALK, THE INTERNET CHAT CHANNEL SPONSORED BY QUILT MAGAZINE
http://www.quilttalk.com/paperpiece/ppdir.html

FOUNDATION PIECING FROM THE WORLD WIDE QUILT PAGE
http://www.quilt.com/Foundations/Foundations.html

MARY GRAHAM DESIGNS' FOUNDATION PAPER-PIECING INSTRUCTIONS
http://www.nmia.com/~mgdesign/qor/pfp.htm

PAPER PANACHE PIECING TUTORIALS AND PATTERNS
http://www.PAPERPANACHE.com/

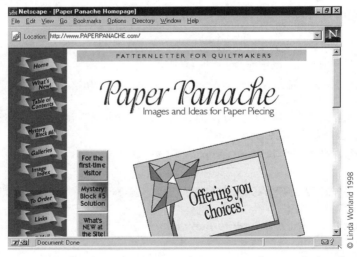

Linda Worland offers everything you need to get started paper piecing, from lessons to tips and ideas.

A PAPER-PIECING LESSON FROM ZIPPY DESIGNS
http://www.other-world.com/ftp/quiltersweb/QSchool/GInstructions.html

PAT COULTER'S ONLINE FRIGID PIECING CLASS FOR PIECING QUILTS WITH IRREGULAR AND THREE-DIMENSIONAL SHAPES
http://www.csrlink.net/users/coulter/FRCLASS.HTM

"PIECING CURVES WITHOUT GOING AROUND THE BEND" BY JOANNA BARNES
http://wso.williams.edu/~jbarnes/quilting/curves.htm

QUILT BLOCK CUT AND SEW LESSONS FROM #QUILTTALK
http://www.quilttalk.com/lessons.html

 Free Border How-tos

ALANA CONEEN SHOWS YOU HOW TO MITER
http://www.mk.net/~coneen/quilters/howto/miter.html

JINNY BEYER SHOWS YOU HOW TO USE BORDERS
http://www.jinnybeyer.com/blocks/main07.html

JINNY BEYER TEACHES SOFT EDGE PIECING
http://www.jinnybeyer.com/tips/tip15-1.html

Jinny Beyer reveals quilting secrets and writes eloquent advice on her Web site.

"JOANNA'S MIGHTY SUSPECT MAGIC MITERING METHOD" BY JOANNA BARNES

http://wso.williams.edu/~jbarnes/quilting/mit_hard.htm

MARY GRAHAM GIVES A LESSON IN PRAIRIE POINT BORDERS

http://www.nmia.com/~mgdesign/qor/prpnts.htm

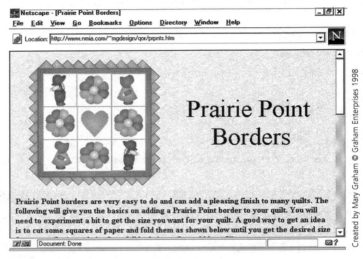

Mary Graham offers many excellent quilting tutorials.

 ### Free Quilt Assembly How-Tos

HAND QUILTING TIPS FROM QUILTNET, COURTESY OF WORLD WIDE QUILTING PAGE

http://ttsw.com/HowTo/HandQuiltingHowTo.html

HOW TO BASE A QUILT, COMPILED FROM QUILTNET, AOL QUILTERS AND USENET MESSAGES, COURTESY OF WORLD WIDE QUILTING PAGE

http://ttsw.com/HowTo/BastingPage.html

Free Quilt Binding and Finishing How-Tos

HOW TO MAKE A HANGING SLEEVE FOR A QUILT FROM MARY GRAHAM DESIGNS
http://wwwnmia.com/~mgdesign/qor/hang.htm

JULIE COGHILL SHARES HER BINDING TIPS
http://www2.polarnt.com/~rcoghill/binding.html

 Free Appliqué How-Tos

"APPLIQUÉ, THE 'A' WORD SIMPLIFIED" BY ADDY HARKAVY FROM QUILT GALLERY MAGAZINE
http://www.quiltgallery.com/technique3.htm

HAND APPLIQUÉ, FREEZER PAPER APPLIQUÉ, AND MACHINE APPLIQUÉ WITH FUSIBLE WEB INSTRUCTIONS FROM QUILT CREATIONS IN FRANCE
http://www.quilt creations.com/applique.htm

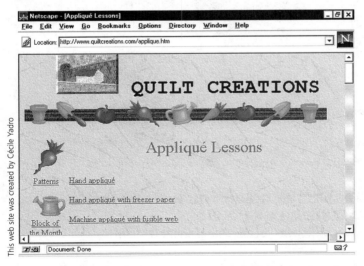

This appliqué tutorial will come to your computer all the way from France! It's by Quilt Creations and is available for reading on their Web site.

**Free Instructions on Assembling
Specific Types of Quilts**

JAN T. SHOWS YOU HOW TO DESIGN AN AMISH-STYLE QUILT WITH ELECTRIC QUILT, COURTESY OF DOWN UNDER QUILTERS ONLINE IN AUSTRALIA
http://www.duquilts.com.au/shopping/duqshop/4elect.htm

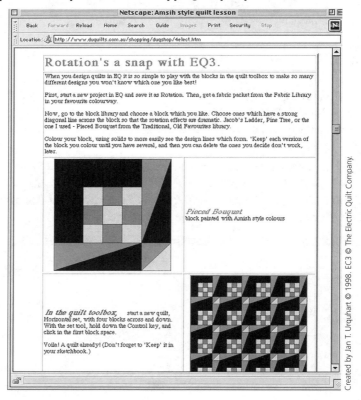

JINNY BEYER SHOWS YOU HOW TO MAKE A PALETTE CHARM QUILT
http://www.jinnybeyer.com/blocks/main13.html

GRADUATED FABRIC DYEING
http://kathkwilts.com/lessons/dying.shtml

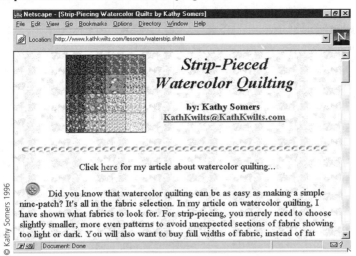

You'll find lots of marvelous tutorials at Kathy Somer's quilting Web site. Many are written by Kathy, but many are written by her talented friends.

POAKALANI SHOWS YOU HOW TO MAKE A HAWAIIAN QUILT
http://www.poakalani.com/frame/quilt2.htm

"TEN TIPS FOR CREATING A SIGNATURE QUILT" BY ELIZABETH P. WILLIAMS
http://members.aol.com/heart2hnd/Index.htm

What's a Web channel?

"Channel" is an Internet buzzword with several meanings. The latest versions of Netscape and Internet Explorer offer channel features that regularly download news, features, stock prices, and sports scores.

Navigator's channel feature is called Netcaster, and to access it press Ctrl-8 while connected to the Web. In Explorer click the Channels icon. Some of the channels that one can access with Explorer include Disney and National Geographic. Netcaster accesses NBC News and CNN. Some new computers also come with a channel button pad already installed on the screen. But don't confuse these with TV channels. Think of them more like electronic magazines.

Another kind of Web channel is provided by "Webcasters." A popular one is Pointcast. (You can download it for free at **http://www.pointcast.com.**) Pointcast similarly downloads news and features to your computer, but like other Webcasters it has the tendency to take over your computer, flashing ads and dialing the Internet when you'd rather be using your computer for other things.

We think that both Webcasters and the channel features found in browsers are generally impractical for most home computer users.

A more practical kind of Web "channel" is a free personalization service like My Excite (**http://my.excite.com**).

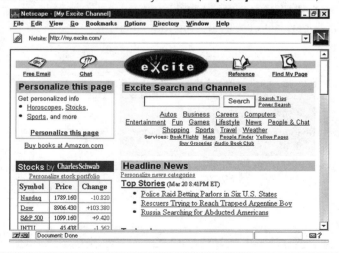

You register on the Web site by filling out a questionnaire. Then you select publications you'd like to read, as well as the sorts of news stories, sports scores, etc. You can also add links to your favorite Web sites. The service creates a personal publication for you that's updated daily. Another good personalization service is Reader's Digest's LookSmart (**http://mulwala.looksmart.com**).

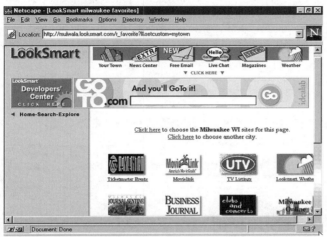

At Reader's Digest's LookSmart you can create a personal Web page that includes newspapers, weather reports, and sports scores specific to the city where you live. You can also add your favorite magazines to the menu.

You can set up your browser to automatically display and update your personal "channel" page. In Netscape 4 pull down the Edit menu and head to Preferences. After "Navigator Starts With" place a dot beside "Home Page." Under Home Page further below, type the URL after Location:. When you're on the Web, press Netscape's Home button to head to the page.

In Internet Explorer 4, pull down the View menu and click Internet Options. Under the General Tab, head to Home Page, and after "Address" type the URL. Click OK to apply.

more free Quilting Tips

CHAPTER 5

Lots of quilting Web sites offer ever-changing rosters of quilting tips and tutorials. Quilt magazines, craft book publishers, vendors of quilting tools and patterns—they're all on the Web offering help, inspiration, and whimsy to quilters. Internet-based quilting discussion groups similarly post regular collections of advice that members have shared. Surfing from one Web site to another, reading these bits of wisdom is like flipping through your favorite quilting magazine. Needless to say, it's an easy way to lose several hours.

#QUILTCHAT IRC CHANNEL QUILT LESSONS
http://kathkwilts.com/lessons

© Kathy Somers 1996

You don't have to tap into an Internet chat channel to read the quilting techniques shared by the members of Kathy Somers' #QuiltChat channel. Lessons include: How to build a floor frame, Dresden Plate directions, mastering borders, and more.

HOW TO KEEP YOUR EDGES STRAIGHT, HOW TO DESIGN A QUILTER'S FLANNEL WALL, AND MORE FROM CHESHIRE CRAFTS
http://www.cheshcat.com/crafts/quilting/quilting.htm

Sally Kosh offers some well-needed tutorials at her homey site.

CANDY GOFF'S HANDQUILTER PAGE
http://www.handquilter.com/

Candy Goff pieces and quilts her quilts entirely by hand, and on her Web site she shares her special methods.

DAVID K. SMALL'S QUILTER'S TIPS
http://www.ici.net/~quilter/text2.htm

David Small offers a variety of quilt tips and lessons.

DELPHI'S NEEDLE & THREAD FORUM
http://www.delphi.com/needle/

Another spot to visit for patterns and tips.

DELPHI'S QUILTING FORUM
http://www.delphi.com/quilting/

Judy Smith's quilters on the Delphi online service offer lots of great tips, patterns, and an ever-changing collection of articles.

DOLL STREET: HOME OF THE DOLL STREET DREAMERS DOLL CLUB
http://www.dolltropolis.com/dollstreet/index.htm

Doll Street offers lots of tips and tutorials on face-painting, stuffing fingers and toes, and improving doll lips. You'll find many in their FAQ archive (**http://www.dolltropolis.com/dollstreet/archives.htm**), *but you should explore the site because lots of information can be found everywhere on it. Doll Street also offers lessons via e-mail. The site is the work of Molly Finnegan, Lori Scianna, Vivienne Stewart, Abby Cohen-Conn, Jim Winer, and many other dollmakers.*

DOWN UNDER QUILTERS ONLINE HELP PAGE
http://www.duquilts.com.au/office/helppage.htm

Australian quilters offer solutions to Web surfing quilters' most frequently asked questions.

GLENDA SCOTT'S FABRIC ORIGAMI WORKSHOP
http://www.owt.com/gdscott/

This is one cool site! Take the ideas behind paper origami and apply them to fabric. Embellish your fabric origami with beads and embroidery. Glenda calls fabric origami a "quilter's dream" for dealing with scraps, and this site will show you what she means.

"HOW TO MAKE SPACE TO QUILT" BY DAWN DUPERAULT
http://www.redsword.com/dduperault/space.htm

Dawn shows you how to make space in your busy home and life for quilting.

🛒 HOW TO UPHOLSTER
http://www.upholster.com/

O.K., it's not exactly a quilting Web site. But there's going to come a day when you stumble on cat-print tapestry fabric that would look perfect on that bedraggled chair in your sewing room. Once you drag home ten pounds of upholstery fabric, you're going to need some guidance on what to do next. You'll find all the help you need at this remarkable site. It tells you how to reupholster everything from ottomans to truck seats, and even sew zippers into pillows.

LESSONS FROM ZSUXXA'S HOUSE
http://zsuxxa@coyote.csusm.edu/public/guests/zsuxxa/

This is a pretty funky site where you can learn how to partipate via e-mail in quilt lessons for projects like a "Kabuki angel."

🛒 MIMI'S HANDBOOK FOR DOLLMAKERS
http://exit109.com/~mimi/handbook/handbook.htm

Dollmaker Gloria J. "Mimi" Winer offers an amazing Web site full of tutorials and advice on face painting, fabrics, body construction, fingers, and more. She has posted several books-worth of advice online that you can read in near totality, including her Handbook for Dollmakers, Mimi's Source List, and her tech guide to resins, rubbers, and clays.

🛒 MRS. SHIELL'S QUILTING SCHOOL
http://www.nettally.com/bjshiell/index.html

Mrs. Shiell shares lessons from the quilting classes she teaches, including instructions for making half-square triangles. She also sells her patterns, templates, and books to accompany the lessons.

🛒 NANCY'S NOTIONS
http://www.nancysnotions.com/SewingRoomLibrary/Library.html

Nancy Zieman of Sewing With Nancy fame offers free lessons and project sheets on her information-rich Web site.

NEEDLEWORK TIPS AND TRICKS
http://www.serve.com/marbeth/tips.html

On Martha Beth Lewis's Piano, Needlework, and Chocolate Home Page you'll find enough quilt tricks to stuff a piano bench—how to block needlework, how to find out-of-print patterns, how to keep knots under control, and much more. Much of this lovely site relates to embroidery, but quilters will find lots of help here too.

PATCHWORDS' QUILTING TIPS AND HOW-TOS
http://www.patchwords.com/departments/tips.html

*This is a wonderful and growing collection of advice and techniques from the folks at Patchwords. Also take a look at the Best Of Patchwords page (**http://www.patchwords.com/ofeatures/bestof. html**) for a selection of many of the great how-to articles that have run on the Web site.*

PAULA MILNER'S SEWING TECHNIQUES
http://www.cyberport.net/users/milnerwm/Instructions.html

Paula shares tutorials on piecing Flying Geese blocks, continuous bias strips, and more.

QUILT GALLERY MAGAZINE
http://www.quiltgallery.com/

Quilt Gallery Magazine is a free quilting magazine that can be read only on the Web. It's full of how-to articles—beautifully written and illustrated.

QUILT MAGAZINE
http://www.quiltmag.com/lessons.html

Quilt Magazine offers lots of great tutorials on compelling topics: remember-me signature blocks, "unorthodox appliqué," quick flying geese, and more.

QUILTBEE FABRIC TIPS
http://needlearts.dm.net/quiltbee/qbfabtip.htm

Here's a selection of tips shared by members of QuiltBee, a quilting mailing list discussion group (see Chapter 15 for information on how to sign up), and compiled by Addy Harkavy.

QUILTER'S NEWSLETTER ONLINE
http://www.quiltersnewsletter.com/rodledit/html/tip922.htm

You'll find some terrific how-tos and tips on this Web site, from the publisher of everyone's favorite quilting magazine.

QUILTING LESSONS FROM DEBBY'S QUILTAHOLICS WEB SITE
http://home1.gte.net/debbyk/lessons.htm

From Debby K.'s Quiltaholics Web site comes a selection of delight-ful quilting lessons.

QUILTING TIPS FROM JINNY BEYER
http://www.jinnybeyer.com/tips.html

Master quilter Jinny Beyer shares lots of quilting tips.

RITA DENENBERG'S QUILTING HOW-TOS
http://www.hypermart.net/myquilts/projects.htm

Rita shows you how to make continuous tube bias binding, how to master freezer paper appliqué, and paper piecing. She has some great original patterns on her site, including one for a cool cat and a gorgeous swan.

SEWING ROOM SET UP HOW-TO
http://www.cheshcat.com/crafts/quilting/q_sewrm.htm

Here's an interesting FAQ file that many quilters on the Net have contributed to. It is maintained by Sally Kosh of the Cheshire's Crafts and Cuisine Web site. It covers sewing room lighting, optimal cutting board and table height, and flooring recommendations.

SUE TRAUDT'S WORLD WIDE QUILTING PAGE HOW-TOS
http://ttsw.com/HowToPage.html

You'll find lots and lots—and lots of advice here about block and foundation piecing, rotary cutting, speed cutting, appliqué, hand and machine quilting, bindings, basting, and more. Take a look at the following World Wide Quilting pages too:

- ### World Wide Quilting Page Hints
  http://quilt.com/Hints.html

  Visitors to the site post their best tips.

- ### World Wide Quilting Page Miscellaneous Help
  http://ttsw.com/MiscQuiltingPage.html

  You'll find more interesting stories, ideas, and quilting insights on this part of the Web site.

SUNBONNET SLEUTH'S QUILTING LESSONS
http://www.mindspring.com/~quiltmag/mystery/contents.html

Sunbonnet Sleuth, a regular guest in the #QuiltTalk chat channel (see Chapter 15 for directions on how to join the chat), offers a series of mystery quilts with quilting lessons.

TEN BASIC LESSONS FROM KWIK SQUARES
http://www.mwaz.com/quilt/00_toc.htm

Kwik Squares, of Prescott Valley, Arizona, offers lessons in quilting, block assembly, stitching, sashings, borders, notions, battings, and more. The blocks page is especially helpful.

THE MINING COMPANY
http://quilting.miningco.com/

The Mining Company hosts a wonderful quilt site with weekly features and tips, written by host Susan C. Druding.

THE NATIONAL ONLINE QUILTERS TIPS AND LESSONS
http://www.noqers.org/tips.htm

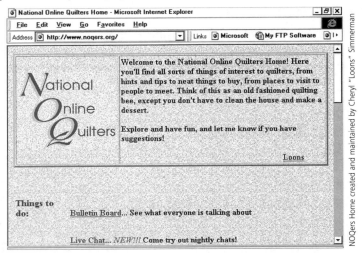

The National Online Quilters is a klatch of quilters that formed years ago on the old online service Delphi (one of the first commercial online services ever). They migrated to the Web under the nurturing guidance of Web hostess Cheryl Simmerman. Their "classroom" page offers montly tips on topics ranging from medallion quilts to quilt tools cat, as well as archives of past tips.

THE USENET TEXTILE FAQS
http://www.lib.ox.ac.uk/internet/news/faq/
rec.crafts.textiles.misc.html

The Textile FAQs are collections of commonly asked questions and answers compiled from the Usenet quilting and sewing newsgroups. They cover everything from book recommendations to quilting advice. You can read them at the above URL at Oxford University's Web site. There are other links to them from various Web sites. A superior link we think can be found at the Needles & Bobbins Thread Store at: **http://www.jcave.com/~dybitter/faqs.html**

THREADS MAGAZINE ONLINE
http://www.taunton.com/th/index.htm

Threads Magazine *offers a wide selection of how-to articles and tips.*

🛒 THE STENCIL COMPANY'S TIPS
http://quiltingstencils.com/ index.html

Created by Holice Turnbow and Donna Logan

You'll find an extensive list of design ideas, tutorials, and answers to frequently asked questions pertaining to stencils. Lots of tips and design ideas for using stencils on the Stencil Co.'s Web site.

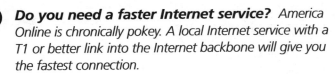

WHY DO SOME WEB PAGES TAKE SO LONG TO DISPLAY?

Some Web pages may take forever to appear because they're full of big pictures and you have a slow modem, but if you find yourself regularly going for coffee as Web pages slowly display, it may be time to investigate other culprits.

Do you need a faster Internet service? *America Online is chronically pokey. A local Internet service with a T1 or better link into the Internet backbone will give you the fastest connection.*

Do you need a faster modem? *These days a 56K bps modem is de rigueur.*

Is your phone line dysfunctional? *Some surfers discover that a chronically sluggish Internet connection is the fault of fuzzy local phone lines. The culprit can be lousy wiring in your house; a "lossy" connector at the phone companies' box; or noise injected on the phone line somewhere between your house and the phone company's substation, usually by repeaters (a common suburban problem). If you suspect a problem, try using your modem to call your Internet service at a neighbor's house and/or an office a few miles away.*

Are you tapping in during rush hours? *Yes, the Internet slows down just like a freeway during certain times of the day. Your ISP can also suffer sluggishness due to heavy use at peak times, like after school, or just before ten p.m. when everyone's dialing to check their e-mail before heading to bed. The solution: set the alarm clock to get your downloading done early in the morning.*

Is your computer hardware at fault? *While faster computers don't translate into faster Internet connections, your computer may be struggling to display Web graphics because of the limited amount of memory on older video cards. If Web page graphics occasionally look smeared across your screen, or scroll-down menu bars tend to disappear in other applications after you've been on the Web, you need a more up-to-date video card.*

free Quilt Fabric and Batting Advice

Remember that first quilt you made—stitched of polyester doubleknit from your dad's leisure suit and snips of wool from your sister's school uniform? Don't tell us that since then you haven't become a bit of, well, a fabric snob. You buy fabric like some buy designer purses, looking for names of designers like Nancy Crow and Jinny Beyer. You indulge in lengthy conversations on the best thread count for muslin. You mull over the properties of different brands of batting with more care than most people expend shopping for a house. If this sounds like you, you're going to love the Internet. That's because there are lots of quilters on it who devote as much passion as you do to shopping for fabric—and they are always eager to share their opinions.

 ## Free Fabric Advice

The best fabric advice you'll find on the Web will come from other quilters. Head to Chapter 15, Free Online Quilting Discussions, to learn how to join the mailing lists where quilters like to hang out. But be warned: sometimes discourse on the merits of different fabric types grows so heated you'll be wishing for a bartender to come and break up the fight—batting is one subject about which arguments tend to get especially out of control. In the meantime, here are Web sites where the fabric advice is a bit more subdued.

BLEEDING FABRIC FAQ
http://ttsw.com/FAQS/BleedingFabricFAQ.htm

This is a compilation of messages from the QuiltNet mailing list containing suggestions on dealing with and preventing fabric bleeding. It comes courtesy of Sue Traudt's World Wide Quilting Web site.

FABRIC STORAGE FAQ
http://www.quilt.com/FAQS/FabricStorageFAQ.html

This is a compilation of advice from the QuiltNet mailing list on how to store fabric. It also comes courtesy of Sue Traudt's World Wide Quilting.

ON-LINE FABRIC DIRECTORY DISCUSSION
http://www.inetcon.com/fabdir.html

Read and post messages about any type of fabric, from upholstery fabric for truck cab seats to Mary Engelbreit prints.

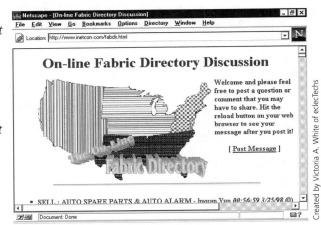

The Internet Connection of Northampton, Massachusetts runs this fascinating site where you can log in to discuss all manner of fabrics, from fabrics in RV's to iridescent taffeta.

TESTING FABRIC FOR FIBER CONTENT
http://www.singersewing.com:80/s-lib1.html

Here's how to do a burn test on fabric to test its fiber content, courtesy of Singer Sewing Machines.

TEXTILE LABELS PROTECT AND INFORM CONSUMERS
http://muextension.missouri.edu/xplor/hesguide/clothing/gh0824.htm

Sharon Stevens, from the department of textile and apparel management, at the University of Missouri, Columbia, offers thorough information on textile labels and what the information means to consumers.

Free Information from Fabric Makers

Several major fabric makers run Web sites where you can find information on their fabric lines, free patterns, a database of stores that carry different lines (a big help when you're trying to locate specific fabric), general fabric advice and in some cases even message areas where you can search for other quilters who may have an extra quarter-yard of that discontinued fabric you need to finish your quilt.

Start your fabric hunting by heading to the **FABRIC MANUFACTURER'S FAQ** on Sue Traudt's World Wide Quilting site. **http://ttsw.com/FAQS/FabricCompaniesFAQ.html**

This is a directory of fabric makers and their addresses that has been compiled by members of the QuiltNet mailing list.

BENARTEX QUILT FABRICS
http://www.benartex.com

RJR FASHION FABRICS
http://www.rjrfabrics.com/

RJR offers a message board to help quilters locate fabric that they may have run out of and which is no longer manufactured.

Racing Around Looking for Fabric to Finish a Quilt? You know the sick feeling: You need just a smidgin of a particular print to finish piecing a quilt, but your quilt store no longer carries it. Head to Pat Knox's Missing Fabric Page **(http://www.knoxgroup.com/missing-fabrics/Default. htm)** to locate other quilters who may have that little piece you need.

Web Auctions Offer Great Fabric Buys. Web auction sites can be a great place to pick up some fabric finds. You'll find lots of chunks of fabric from garage sales and estates at the Ebay Web Auction site **(http://www.ebay.com)**--head to Chapter 12, Free Quilting History Lessons, to learn more about it. To bid on remnants from garment factories (and by remnants we mean, say, 1000 yards or so), head to the Fabric Auction Web site **(http://www.apparelex.com/marketplace/)**. You can bid on everything from seersucker to cotton prints. Unfortunately the minimum bid order is usually 100 yards, but at $1 or so per yard, it's an affordable proposition if you need to sew lots of baby quilts.

 **Battings**

Like we said, batting discussions on the Web can grow tense, especially when the all-cotton camp goes into combat with the cotton-poly blend camp. Our advice? Don't tell anyone the fiber content of the batting you use until you really know who your friends are.

BATTING FAQ, *from QuiltNet, courtesy of Sue Traudt*
http://ttsw.com/FAQS/BattingFAQ.html

BATTING REVIEW, *by Addy Harkavy for Patchwords*
http://www.patchwords.com/ofeatures/bats.html

BATTINGS, *Middle Layer Key to the Look of Your Quilt, by Addy Harkavy for Planet Patchwork*
http://tvq.com/batting.htm

MOUNTAIN MIST
http://www.palaver.com/mountainmist/prshow/welcome.htm
Mountain Mist gives free advice on its Web site. This batting manufacturer offers care advice as well as quilting information.

WARM AND NATURAL: IDEAS AND TIPS
http://www.warmcompany.com/ideastips.htm

The Warm Company, manufacturer of Warm and Natural batts, explains how give your quilts an antique look with batting.

 *More Than You Ever Wanted to Know About Cotton?* Do you ever lay awake at night worried about the world's cotton supply? Concerned that there might not be enough when you finally get around to finishing all those quilt tops in your closet? You can read everything you've ever wanted to know about cotton supply and distribution at the Web site of the International Cotton Advisory Committee (**http://www.icac.org/icac /english/ main.html**). *King Cotton Magazine* (**http://www.cotton.net/**), published by the manufacturer of the same name will tell you even more about cotton.

Free Quilt Shopping Directories

There are a bizillion quilt shops on the Web. Here are directories to help you find them, both on the Web and in your city— or the city you travel to.

BUYER'S INDEX FOR SEWING, FABRICS AND TEXTILES
http://www.buyersindex.com/brca/42.htm

This is a great site to begin your hunt if you're shopping for certain fabrics, notions, books, and threads. It offers a searchable database.

LANCASTER COUNTY, PENNSYLVANIA FABRIC SHOPS
http://www.quiltart.com/lancaster.html

Judy Smith has compiled this list of all the quilting-related shops and other touristy spots you'll want to visit should you head to the quilt show in Lancaster. It even includes a map and directions.

LET'S GO QUILT SHOPPING
http://www.quiltmag.com/links/linkstoqltshop.html

Compiled by Quilt Magazine, *this site features a nice collection of links to quilt shops with web pages.*

QUILT SEARCH
http://www.quiltsearch.com/Quilt/index.html

This is a huge database of quilt stores, manufacturers, and suppliers. You can search by a zip code or by using all or part of a company name.

QUILT SHOPS AROUND THE WORLD
http://www.paston.co.uk/natpat/overshop.html

From That Patchwork Association in the United Kingdom comes this traveler's directory to quilt stores in foreign lands.

 # Quilting Thread, Notions, and Tools Advice

Where would we quilters be without our shelves and baskets full of quilting gadgets: the rotary cutters, marking pencils, glue sticks, rulers, and thimbles? It surprises us that some enterprising soul doesn't sell tool belts for quilters. Here's some of the advice on using and selecting quilting tools that you'll find on the Web. Need to know the best marking pencil, the right needle for the job? Searching for directions on how to build your own quilt frame? You'll find it all on some of these Web sites.

QUILTING TOOLS AND NOTIONS
FROM WIDE WORLD QUILTING PAGE
http://ttsw.com/QuiltingTools.html

Sue Traudt offers a library of information on hoops, frames, notions, wall hangers, stencils, batting, and tools for cutting and marking. Much of the advice has been compiled from conversations on the QuiltNet mailing list and the Usenet group rec.crafts.quilting.

 ## *Free Needle Advice*

WHEN IS A NEEDLE MORE THAN A NEEDLE?
http://tvq.com/needles.htm

The ever-audacious Rob Holland attacks this prickly subject.

Head to Free Help for Sewing Machines, Chapter 13, for Web sites that will help you untangle such dilemmas as to why your sewing-machine thread keeps breaking.

Free Thread Advice

"THREAD FACT" BY ROSE MARIE TONDL
AND WENDY RICH
http://www.ianr.unl.edu/pubs/NebFacts/nf91-37.htm

Rose and Wendy, from the University of Nebraska Cooperative Extension, share their knowledge about the many different types of threads on the market, plus offer tips, care, and a selection guide in this Web brochure.

THREAD TALES & TIPS
http://pages.prodigy.com/sewsomething/thread.htm

Sheree KcKee has authored and compiled this guide for the Sew Something Exciting Web site.

 Web Homes of Thread and Ribbon Makers that Offer Free Projects and Advice

🛒 COATS AND CLARK
http://www.coatsandclark.com/

From the maker of Anchor, Dual Duty Plus and other threads, this Web site offers free advice plus a free stuff link.

DMC
http://www.dmc-usa.com/

The DMC page offers many free projects and information on all the DMC threads, a history of DMC, and "Project Central"—home to free projects.

KREINIK MANUFACTURING COMPANY, INC.
http://www.kreinik.com/t&yguide.htm

Kreinik provides a nice guide to using metallic threads.

MADEIRA THREAD
http://www.pacificharbor.com/scs/

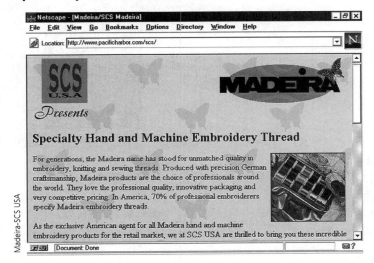

Tap into the Web sites of thread makers for tips on using their threads, plus project directions and ideas. You'll read interesting hand and machine embroidery thread advice here—and lots of sewing and craft tips. Share a tip of your own and you could win a Madeira thread gift box.

OFFRAY RIBBON
http://www.offray.com/prod.html

There is product information, history, and how-to information on topics such as making bows, holiday ornaments, Victorian ornaments and accessories, plus directions for a brocade pillow and lampshade at this lavish site. If you like ribbonwork, you'll love the free patterns here.

SULKY OF AMERICA
http://www.sulky.com/

The Sulky Web site offers advice on using Sulky threads, plus a monthly free project.

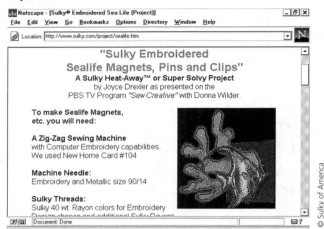

 Free Advice on Quilting Hoops and Frames

"BEYOND THE LAP HOOP" BY ADDY HARKAVY
http://tvq.com/frames.htm

Addy Harkavy wrote this essay for Planet Patchwork.

HOW TO MAKE A FLOOR QUILT FRAME
http://kathkwilts.com/lessons/flframe.shtml

Kathy Somers of KathKwilts offers directions on building your own.

HOW TO MAKE A QUILT HOOP STAND
http://www.quilt.com/miscquilting/hoopstanddirections.html

Susan M. (she doesn't give her last name) provides these directions.

QUILTING FRAMES AND HOOPS
http://ttsw.com/Tools/HoopsAndFrames.html

Sue Traudt and the World Wide Quilting Web site offer this compilation of addresses of quilt frame and hoop makers, and advice that has been posted as messages in the QuiltNet mailing list, the newsgroup rec.crafts.quilting, and the America Online quilting forum.

Free Advice on Quilting Tools

🛒 AMERICAN TRADITIONAL STENCILS
http://www.Amtrad-stencil.com/

Want to learn how to use stencils to emboss? This site includes a marvelous projects page.

EZ INTERNATIONAL TOOL TUTORIAL
http://www.ezquilt.com/tutorial.html

Learn how to cut hexagons, equilateral triangles, triangles, and diamonds at this well-illustrated site.

FISKAR SCISSORS
http://www.fiskars.com/start.html

At the Web site of this scissors maker you'll find free craft products and snipping advice.

KWIK SQUARES - THE TRIANGLE SQUARE CALCULATOR DEMO PAGE
http://www.mwaz.com/quilt/calculat.htm

Kwik Squares offers a nifty explanation of making quick-pieced triangle units from squares.

MARKING PENCIL INFORMATION
http://www.prairienet.org/community/clubs/quilts/pencils.html

Read some casual test results of using various fabric marking pencils. This was originally posted to the Usnet newsgroup rec.crafts.textiles.quilting.

🛒 NANCY'S NOTIONS
http://www.nancysnotions.com/

You can't go wrong tapping into this site, where you'll find advice on anything sewing-related you can imagine.

THE STENCIL COMPANY
http://quiltingstencils.com/index.html

The Stencil Company answers lots of quilt design questions, many having to do with stencils, on topics like quilting concentric circles, set-in piecing techniques, and quilting Celtic patterns.

free Quilt Embellishment How-Tos

Be honest: you don't really want someone to sit on your quilt, do you? You want to be-ribbon it, be-bow it, bead it, embroider it, and festoon it with lace, buttons, charms, rick-rack, and all manner of gew-gaws. There are many Web sites dedicated to helping you achieve embellishment excess on your quilts. So many that we've decided to devote an entire chapter to them. Some of these sites are specifically for quilters, others are geared for practitioners of embroidery and beading. We've also added a few sites for lacemakers for quilters who like to stitch crochet and other lace into their projects.

 ## Web Crazy Quilting Mania!

They're everywhere on the Web, spreading their enthusiasm for quilts without any plan or orderly design. That's not surprising since the Web is itself a crazy quilt of jagged intentions and kaleidoscopic colors. Who better to populate it than crazy quilters?

THE CRAZY QUILT MAILING LIST
http://www.quiltropolis.com/

Conceived by Dawn Smith and run by Beth Ober of Quiltropolis, this bubbly group of crazy quilt fans discusses hand and machine embroidery on quilts; lace, bead, button and ribbon embellishment; books and classes on crazy quilts, and more. To sign up head to Quiltropolis.

THE CRAZY QUILT SOCIETY
http://www.crazyquilt.com/

The Crazy Quilt Society is a program of the Quilt Heritage Foundation. Membership is $25 per year. Benefits include a newsletter and annual conferences. Esteemed members include Judith Baker Montano, Penny McMorris, Leslie Levison, and Cindy Brick (newsletter editor).

(Note: In Chapter 12, Free Quilting History Lessons, you'll find links to crazy quilt history sites on the Web.)

VINTAGE VOGUE CRAZY QUILT GALLERY
http://www.vintagevogue.com/html/crazy_quilting.html

Vintage Vogue offers a gallery of links to the Web sites of
crazy-quilters and their work all around the Web.

Free Embroidery Lessons and Tips

ELIZABETHAN BLACKWORK
http://www.pobox.com/~pkm/bwarch.html

*The Elizabethan
Blackwork Web
site offers lots
of beautiful free
patterns created
by Paula Katherine
Marmor.*

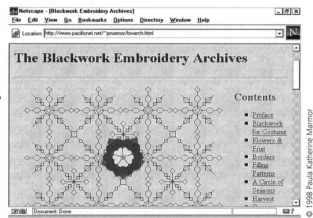

© 1998 Paula Katherine Marmor

THE EMBROIDERY MALL
http://www.EmbroideryMall.com/

*The Embroidery
Mall offers infor-
mation and sup-
plies, plus links to
an embroidery
e-mail discussion
list. You'll find
information on
supplies, free
designs, lots of
articles on
embroidery, and
an embroidery*

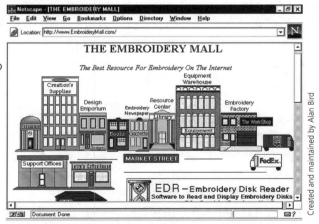

Created and maintained by Alan Bird

discussion group. Take a look at the Embroidery Mall's library **(http://www.
embroiderymall.com/library/)** *for a thread database and much more.*

KATHLEEN DYER'S COUNTED CROSS STITCH, NEEDLEWORK, AND STITCHERY PAGE
http://www.wco.com/~kdyer/xstitch.html

This is a fantastic Web site with links to embroidery information all over the Internet, plus free tutorials and charts.

MEDIEVAL EMBROIDERY
http://www.tiac.net/users/drbeer/joyce/emb/embroid.htm

Joyce Miller offers free charts that you can print plus insights into embroidery by our ancestors.

SHARON BOGGON'S NEEDLEWORK STITCH DICTIONARY
http://online.anu.edu.au/english/jems/sharon/stitchdictionary contents.html

Sharon, in Canberra, Australia, offers a large and beautifully illustrated Web-based embroidery stitch dictionary in which you can look up tutorials for specific stitches. She asks that users in "shareware payment" mail her something from their scrap bag.

USENET NEEDLEWORK FAQ: FLOSS, FIBERS AND THREADS
http://www.wco.com/~kdyer/documents/nf_fibers.html

Kathleen Dyer compiles this indispensable guide to "frequently asked questions" in the rec.crafts.textiles.needlework newsgroup. It covers everything from floss choices to color bleeding.

 Free Ribbon Help

THE CHARTED DESIGNERS OF AMERICA
http://www.stitching.com/CDA/ribspidr.htm

You'll find lots of instructions and illustrations on perfecting your ribbon embroidery stitches.

HOW TO MAKE DIMENSIONAL OR RUCHED FLOWERS, FROM SUE TRAUDT'S WORLD WIDE QUILTING WEB SITE
http://ttsw.com/Bernina/Challenge96/Lesson5.html

OFFRAY RIBBON HOW-TOS
http://www.offray.com/

Offray Ribbon offers a bunch of how-tos on creating ribbon flowers, decorating boxes, embellishing bridalwear and more.

THE PIECEMAKERS SILK RIBBON EMBROIDERY FAQ
http://www.piecemakers.com/free/silk_faq.html

 ## *Free Beading Help*

THE BEADWORKER
http://exo.com/~emily/beadworker.html

Emily Hackbarth's site offers lots of tips, project, tutorials, and links to other beading Web sites. There's even special beading graph paper that you can print.

BEAD NET
http://www.mcs.net/~simone/beadnet.html

Bead Net, by Simone Oettinger, offers an incredible library of information on beading including advice on selecting and using beads, links to other beading sites and manufacturers' Web sites (like a company that offers "beaded appliqués"), plus a "cyber-bead embroiderers" page.

BEAD TALK MAILING LIST DISCUSSION GROUP
http://www.quiltropolis.com/

Cindy's Crafts and Quiltropolis sponsor an e-mail based discussion list devoted to discussing all aspects of beading and related crafts. To join head to Quiltropolis' Web site.

KAREN A. LAMBERT'S BEADING WEB SITE
http://members.aol.com/KALDesign/beads.html

When it comes to stitching pearls on crazy quilts, not just any pearls will do! Read lots of good advice from Karen on selecting beads to stitch on your quilt.

Free Lace-Making Tutorials and Advice

THE LACEMAKER'S HOME PAGE
http://www.arachne.com/

Liz Reynolds introduces you to the art of lace-making and offers links to other lace-related sites on the Web.

THE LEGACY OF LACE
http://www.legacyoflace.com/

Lace expert Joeanna Smith offers discussion and illustration of the history of European needle and bobbin laces, like 17th-century point de neige.

 ## Free General Needlework Tips

"NEEDLEWORK ON-LINE SOURCES & SUPPLIERS," BY DEBI MCMAHON
http://www.crl.com/~dmcmahon/sources.html

Debi offers a comprehensive list of retailers and manufacturers on the Web who sell often hard-to-find stitching items like overdyed floss and beads.

🛒 THE NEEDLEARTS MALL
http://www.needlearts.com/shop_index.html

Although this is a commercial site, with links to embroidery-related retailers, it's nearly a magazine with articles on different aspects of stitching, tutorials, lessons, and much more.

🛒 WONDERFUL STITCHES WWW
http://www.needlework.com/

You'll find lots of information on cross-stitch, quilting, needlepoint, and other decorative forms of stitching.

free Advice on Quilt Cleaning, Storage, and Appraisal

Who doesn't want to display their beautiful quilts for all the world to see? But where and how you display them can mean all the difference in how well they hold up over time. Sunlight is your quilt's worst enemy, but there are others like sweaty hands and stains. Many Web sites offer free advice on repairing, cleaning, and storing quilts. Some sites also offer advice on obtaining appraisals of quilts for insurance. Our favorite sites are the stain removal ones where you specify a stain and the site tells you how to remove it.

 Free Quilt Storage, Cleaning, and Conservation Advice

"CARING FOR ANTIQUE QUILTS" BY BARB VAN VIERZEN
http://www.kawartha.net/~jleonard/quilts.htm

From the Peterborough Centennial Museum and Archives comes advice on storing, airing, and cleaning old quilts (and photographs).

CARYL FALLERT'S SHIPPING, HANGING & STORAGE TIPS
http://www.bryerpatch.com/faq/storage.htm

Well-known quilter Caryl Fallert reveals how she stores, ships, and hangs her precious quilts. Coming soon: directions from Caryl for making a shipping tube.

"CONSERVATION OF TEXTILE ITEMS" BY SHIRLEY NIEMEYER AND PATRICIA COX CREWS
http://www.ianr.unl.edu/pubs/NebFacts/nf93-137.htm

The University of Nebraska Extension article offers extensive advice on cleaning, care, storage, and display of treasured textiles.

CONSERVATION HANDOUTS
FROM THE BISHOP MUSEUM IN HAWAII
http://www.bishop.hawaii.org/bishop/conservation/conservation.html

Bishop Museum publishes a variety of pamphlets on conservation, and many are available for reading on its Web site. Among them: "Bugs Are Eating My Family Treasures," "Wet Cleaning Quilts at Home," "Care of Feathers," "Archival Mounts For Paintings on Textiles," "Bleaching," and "Caring for Tapa." The museum also offers books on conservation that one could order.

"THE DISPLAY AND CARE OF ART QUILTS"
BY APRIL NIINO, PENNY NII QUILT ART
http://206.204.3.133/dir_nii/nii_dat_quicar.html

The Penny Nii gallery offers advice on hanging, storing, and cleaning quilts, as well as combatting the effects of sunlight.

"HOW DO I STORE ANTIQUE TEXTILES AT HOME?"
BY THE SMITHSONIAN
http://160.111.7.240/resource/faq/nmah/antqtext.htm

The Smithsonian offers free advice on storing a variety of antique textiles at home, including quilts but also tapestries, rugs, and costumes.

"HOW TO CARE FOR VICTORIAN SILK QUILTS
AND SLUMBER THROWS," BY THE SMITHSONIAN
http://160.111.7.240/resource/faq/nmah/vicquilt.htm

Learn the best way to care for lavishly stitched Victorian needlework, including how to repair, clean, and store it.

ILLINI COUNTRY STITCHERS' TEXTILE PRESERVATION
RESOURCES (ESPECIALLY FOR QUILTERS)
http://www.prairienet.org/community/clubs/quilts/pres.html
and http://www.prairienet.org/quilts/preserve.html

The Champaign, Illinois quilt guild offers a list of Web sites devoted to textile preservation, and as well as a bibliography of good books on preservation, many published by museums.

Download Acrobat to Read Online Brochures.
Many universities and government agencies publish brochures on the Web in a desktop publishing format called PDF for "portable document format." In order to read them you'll need to download and install the free Acrobat reader from Adobe Systems (**http://www.adobe.com**). Once you install it, whenever your Web browser encounters a PDF file on a Web page, it will automatically fire up Acrobat and display the brochure for you just as it would look if you ordered it from the agency.

KANSAS STATE UNIVERSITY'S CLOTHING AND TEXTILE LIBRARY
http://129.130.75.14/library/PUB/LIBRARY/clothtxt/cltxtpub.htm

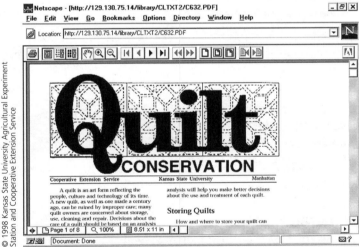

Kansas State offers online versions of many of its publication on quilt conservation. In addition, it offers a fascinating library of textile-related pamphlets and articles, including one on disinfecting textiles. To read them you'll need a copy of Adobe Acrobat (see Tip above).

🛒 THE KIRK COLLECTION
http://206.138.137.9/kirk/main2.htm

You'll find lots of information on quilt care and conservation on this Web site of The Kirk Collection in Omaha, Nebraska. Kirk specializes in mail-order sales of reproduction fabrics, conservation products like acid-free tissue and storage boxes, and books on quilt restoration and conservation. The company also sponsors a Quilt Restoration Society and conferences.

PRESERVING QUILTS IN YOUR HOME
http://www.dos.state.fl.us/dhr/museum/acs_1.html

The Museum of Florida History offers advice on the care, storage, and display of quilts. They also include a recommended reading list, and list of suppliers of products for archival preservation.

"QUILT CARE 101" BY DAVID K. SMALL
http://home.ici.net/quilter/text11.htm

Here's an amusing and informative article on how to take good care of a quilt—with warnings not to toss it in the washing machine and other silly things.

QUILT STORAGE AND DISPLAY ADVICE FROM DAWN DUPERAULT
http://www.redsword.com/dduperault/storage.htm

Dawn Duperault offers considerable advice on storing and displaying quilts for posterity.

THE QUILTBROKER
http://www.quiltbroker.com/quilt_storage.html

Should you wrap your quilts in buffered or unbuffered acid-free tissue? Should you store your quilts on tubes? The QuiltBroker answers such questions and many more on its quilt storage information page. The company also sells acid-free tissue and boxes, and care labels.

WORLD WIDE QUILTING WEB SITE QUILT CARE ADVICE
http://ttsw.com/HowTo/QuiltCare.html

Sue Traudt's World Wide Quilting Web site offers a collection of ideas and comments on quilt care gathered from members of the Quilt Net mailing list discussion group, AOL Quilters Online, and Usenet. Subjects include washing quilts and handling faded fabrics.

 Free Appraisal Advice

DEBORAH ROBERT'S QUILT APPRAISAL PAGE
http://quilt.com/DebbieRoberts/appraise.htm

Certified quilt appraiser Roberts explains why you should get your quilts appraised and how to hire an appraiser. Her site includes a list of appraisers certified by the American Quilter's Society and who can be e-mailed. These appraisers are qualified to appraise fair market, insurance, and donation values of quilts. Roberts also provides quilt care, labeling, and storage advice.

 Free Stain Removal Help

It's happened to all of us. Your significant other slops spaghetti sauce on your great-grandma's quilt, or a guest plops a taco casserole on your painstakingly hand-pieced table runner. Quick! Before the stain sets, tap into one of these Web sites for directions on stain exorcism. You can also head to any of the major Web searchers like Excite! **(http://www.excite.com)** and type in, say, "ketchup stain" to find Web sites with removal directions. But in all honesty, we still prefer Heloise's well-tested stain removal tips!

THE FABRICLINK
http://www.fabriclink.com/

Fabric University, sponsored by Monsanto and Amoco Fabrics and Fibers, offers a variety of information on fabrics, fibers, and fabric care (mostly synthetic, not surprisingly). This is where you go when you want to find out what those microfiber fabrics are really made of. The Clothing & Fabric Care database (**http://www.fabriclink.com/RF-CARE.html**) *offers realms of fabric cleaning advice. You can get the lowdown on fabric flammability issues and how they relate to your family* (**http://www.fabriclink. com/RF-FLAM.html**). *Fiber University* (**http://www.fabriclink.com/ University.html**) *will fill you in on the fiber history of different synthetics and blends, characteristics, trademarks, and care.*

HI TECH DETERGENTS, LTD.'S STAIN REMOVAL GUIDE
http://www.hitechdeterg.co.nz/frame1.htm

Here's an excellent spot removal guide, from New Zealand soap-maker Hi Tech Detergents. You'll find remedies for hundreds of fabric wreckers from nail polish to ice-cream. The site also offers fabric care advice, and insights into the effects of different kinds of laundering methods, soaps, and detergents on different types of fabric.

MIMI'S HANDBOOK FOR DOLLMAKERS: STAIN REMOVAL CHAPTER
http://exit109.com/~mimi/handbook/handbook.htm

Dollmaker Gloria J. "Mimi" Winer covers chocolate kisses, blood spots, "bear baths," and machine washing.

THE RESOURCE: TEXTILES, CLOTHING & DESIGN
http://www.ianr.unl.edu/pubs/Textiles/

The University of Nebraska Cooperative Extension offers advice on handling the sorts of stains and odors that often infect rural quilts: skunk perfume, pesticide stench, smoke odors, and mildew. The site even offers advice on how to salvage textiles from floods.The university offers online versions of many of its other publications on textile care.

THE TIDE CLOTHESLINE
http://www.clothesline.com/

Calling itself "the most comprehensive site on the Web dedicated to keeping your clothes looking their best," detergent-maker Tide offers an interactive Stain Detective to help you rub out spots. Select your spot maker from a list of hundreds, choose the fabric type, and specify whether it's white or printed. The Stain Detective will come up with a remedy (although washing in Tide is always the last step). Some of the directions advise to merely use "stain remover" but some are pretty clever.

Fabric care tips, garment labeling advice, and tips for keeping childrens' clothes clean are also available. Be careful, though: after visiting this site you may suffer the urge to run to the washing machine and spend the day laundering.

WORLD WIDE QUILTING'S STAIN REMOVAL FAQ
http://quilt.com/FAQS/StainRemovalFAQ.html

Sue Traudt has compiled all the stain removal advice proffered in the QuiltNet mailing list discussion group over the years. Some very good ideas!

free Quilt Design and Drawing How-Tos

The longer you quilt the more you realize how wrong your parents were when they insisted you take algebra instead of art in high school. (Boy, were they ever!) Imagine reaching adulthood and not understanding how to use two-point perspective. Or approaching middle-age thinking that a color wheel is something that happens to your car's hubcaps when you back up over your husband's cans of paint. But it is never too late to remedy the sins of our parents and public education.

Here's a gaggle of Web sites that we think offer valuable remedial education in matters ranging from color selection in quilts to drawing in perspective. Some sites are geared specifically to quilters, while others are for artists in general. We've included a few sites that show one how to draw shapes that many quilters would like to master, like tessellations and Celtic knots.

 Color Help

"BASIC COLOR THEORY" BY DOUGLAS BARKEY
http://exchange.coa.edu/HEJourney/polcom/colort.html

Here's a very good introduction to the color wheel, plus concepts like color hue, saturation, and value.

COLOR FROM THE WEBSTITCHER'S SOURCEBOOK
http://home.earthlink.net/~rcausbrook/color.html

Here's an interesting Web site. R. Causbrook offers insights into colors, plus links to some of the most interesting color-related sites on the Web, like Web coloring book pages (great for appliqué!). She also offers a chart that matches DMC floss colors to HTML color codes (in other words, the colors on Web pages), for cyber-savvy needlework designers.

"COLOR IN QUILTS" BY MARY GRAHAM
http://www.nmia.com/~mgdesign/qor/color.htm

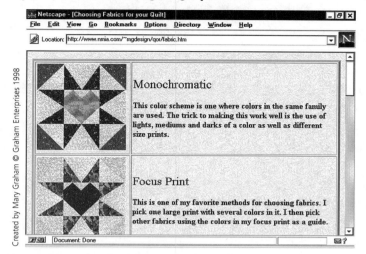

Have problems choosing fabrics and colors without making expensive mistakes? Mary Graham helps quilters master the color wheel, and also offers mini-tutorials on her favorite strategies for choosing quilt colors and prints.

COLOR MATTERS
http://www.lava.net/~colorcom/

If you've ever pondered the psychological implications of your color choices, you'll want to jump into the free-spirited discussions that transpire on this site, devoted to exploring the mysteries of color. Recent topics: why consumers find fast-food most palatable when swaddled in orange and yellow wrappers; why toy collectors prefer red trucks over other colors; whether green chalkboards or black are most conducive to learning.

POYNTON'S COLOR FAQ
http://www.inforamp.net/~poynton/notes/colour_and_gamma/ColorF AQ.html

Once you've read the above primers on color, head to this site for more information on the things that create color intensity, luminance, hue, and saturation.

PSYCHOLOGY OF COLOR FROM FALL RIVER DECORATIVE ARTS
http://fallriver.ns.ca/monthly/colour/moncolo1.htm

Linda Hoffman offers a color quiz to help you explore your feelings about color and choose colors wisely.

REVIEWS OF COLOR IN TEXTILE CRAFTS RESOURCES
http://www.prairienet.org/community/clubs/quilts/color.text.html

Quilters have written lots of books on choosing colors for quilts. This Web site offers terrific and thorough reviews of most of them.

"SPECTRUM COLORS" BY BETSY SZYMANSKI
http://compuquilt.com/rgb.htm

Many quilt design programs let you "mix" colors by adjusting RGB or red-green-blue values. Confused already? Betsy Szymanski offers offers help and explanations.

UNDERSTANDING COLOR
http://humboldt1.com/~color/index.html

How color works is the topic of this wonderful educational Web site designed for "grade 7 and above," but if you're like us you'll appreciate the low-key explanations of lingo like RGB, CMYK, and pigment color.

 Drawing Help

ART STUDIO CHALKBOARD
http://www.saumag.edu/art/studio/chalkboard.html

Catch all those art lessons you missed by tapping into this remarkable art-teaching site by Ralph Larmann, an instructor in Southern Arkansas University's art department. Some lessons: perspective, vanishing points, drawing shadows, shading, composition.

DRAW YOUR OWN CELTIC KNOTWORK
http://home.ctnet.com/drew/knotwork.html

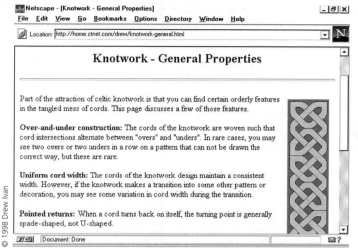

You'll find wonderful directions on how to use graph paper to draw highly geometric spiraling patterns that are perfect to use in quilt designs.
Drew Ivan explains how to draw knotwork—patterns many quilters would like to be better able to draw.

DRAWING FACES
http://susanooh. anime.net/Art /Class/02/index. html

If you sew dolls, as many quilters do, you know that the most critical—and difficult— part is drawing and painting the faces. Japanese animator Hiroyuki Hironaga offers illustrated lessons on planning facial topography and drawing eyes and expressions.

LIFE DRAWING
http://labweb.soemadison.wisc.edu/art332/

Art teacher Robert Gomez fills aspiring quilt artists in on the use of value, texture, shading, and perspective on his art class Web site. An art instructor at University of Wisconsin, Madison, Gomez offers a complete cyber-version of all his figure-drawing classes (ostensibly for students who skipped class, but really for the whole world, he admits). You'll learn about drawing with value, texture, and perspective. You'll learn tricks to check proportions in drawing, and the difference between blind contour drawing and cross contour drawing. The site is lavishly illustrated with works of the masters—and it's lots of fun too.

SUZANNE ALEJANDRE'S TESSELLATION DRAWING TUTORIALS
http://forum.swarthmore.edu/sum95/suzanne/tess.intro.html

Suzanne Alejandre, a Yucaipa, California middle-school math teacher, offers superb step-by-step instructions on drawing tessellations with different drawing programs like Claris Works and PC Paintbrush.

We love to work on our computers and we love stitching, but.... Doing either for long periods can cause repetitive stress injuries like carpal tunnel syndromes. Ignored, repetitive stress injuries can turn into true disabilities. Lots of quilters on the Internet suffer from such maladies. You can read tips on avoiding repetitive stress at Martha Beth Lewis's Web site on Repetitive Stress Injuries and Needlework (**http://www.serve.com/marbeth/needlework_RSI.html**) and at TIFAW (Typing Injury Frequently Asked Questions) (**http://www.tifaw.com**).

Our favorite tip: Staring at your computer for long periods is not good for your eyes. Keep your eyes lubricated by blinking frequently and focusing on other objects.

Our best advice: Take frequent breaks.

free Fabric Dyeing, Painting, Stamping, and Photo-Transferring How-Tos

Sure, billions of bolts of fabric cram the stores, but there are times when you still can't find what you want. If you've ever had a hankering to create your own fabric designs, either through dyeing, painting, and rubber-stamping, or through the magic of your computer printer, there's a Web site out there to help you. As usual, other quilters who've been-there-done-that are your best source of information. Here's how to find them, their advice, and their Web pages.

Free Dyeing Recipes and Advice

A GLIMPSE INTO MARJORIE BEVIS' MARBLING PROCESS
http://www.marbledfabrics.com/aglimpse.htm
Marbling fabric expert Marjorie Bevis offers her own tips and directions.

"HAND MARBLING FOR QUILTERS" BY JANET WICKELL
http://www.UserHome.com/quilting/marble.html

This is the nicest collection of information we've come across on the Web for marbling fabric, selecting paints, tools, and preparing fabric.

© Janet Wickell 1997

🛒 MENDEL'S MARBLE PRINTING ON FABRIC
http://www.mendels.com/marble.html

Mendel's art-supply and fabric store offers dye recipes, directions, tips, and book recommendations for marbling.

QUILTNET ON FABRIC MARBELING
http://quilt.com/FAQS/MarbledFabricFAQ.html

Quilters on the QuiltNet discussion list discuss their tips and techniques for marbling fabric, a compilation courtesy of the World Wide Quilting page.

"THE HISTORY OF MARBLED FABRIC" BY MARJORIE BEVIS
http://www.marbledfabrics.com/history.htm

Marjorie describes her trip to Istanbul to view marbling experts at work.

Don't Feel like Dyeing Fabric Yourself?
Lots of quilters on the Internet sell hand-dyed fabric. Just ask in any of the quilting mailing lists described in Chapter 15 or in the DyersLIST mailing list described on page 108. By the way, Gloria has dyed so much fabric that for the past few years she's kept lots of it in her car. She ran out of storage room in her house. You'll find many quilters in similar circumstances on the Web.

"MAKING SHIBORI FABRIC" BY COZY BENDESKY
http://www.erols.com/cozy/ shibori1.html

Cozy explains in step-by-step directions that include photos how to create shibori fabrics.

Think Twice Before Refusing a Cookie

Are cookies bad for you? We mean the Internet kind, not the kind that disappears into your mouth moments after you pluck it from a bag. Web cookies are bits of code that a Web site sends to your browser so that it can track your activities on the site. Shopping Web sites and big glitzy publications like *The New York Times* rely on cookies to expedite your navigation of their services, and sometimes track your use of the site for marketing purposes. Many people consider cookies violations of privacy. We think such worries are overblown. And no, one Web site can't retrieve from your computer cookies that another Web site has sent you. For the paranoid there are a plethora of cookie blockers, stompers, cutters, and smashers available for downloading from the Web (check the Web site of *PC World* at **http://www.fileworld.com** for the latest). Do we use 'em? Naw. One disadvantage of blocking cookies is that whenever you tap into a Web site that requires a password you have to type it yourself, for your browser won't remember it.

"A SIMPLE METHOD OF ONE-POT, MULTI-COLOR DYEING" BY SUSAN DRUDING AND SUSIE HODGES
http://www.straw.com/sig/multipot.html

Dye experts Susan Druding and Susie Hodges reveal a straightforward recipe for dyeing protein fibers like wool, silk and nylon with acid wool dyes.

"BASIC INSTRUCTIONS FOR WORKING WITH REACTIVE AND WASHFAST ACID DYES" BY PAT WILLIAMS
http://www.art.acad.emich.edu/faculty/williams/basicdyeinstr.htm

Excellent dye recipes from Eastern Michigan University's art department.

🛒 CAROL TODD'S NATURAL DYEING HOMEPAGE
http://www.slonet.org/~crowland/

Carol Todd, author of Earth Tones, Colors from Western Dye Plants, *introduces visitors to the world of natural dyes. She offers lots of links to related Web sites. Be sure to check out her "plant of the month."*

DHARMA TRADING COMPANY
http://www.dharmatrading.com/index.html

Dharma is a great mail-order source for many dyeing supplies and books, and related products. Their Web site occasionally offers good articles.

DRITZ DYEING ADVICE
http://www.dritz.com/projects.html

The Prym-Dritz Corp. tells you how to dye wood and wicker, among other things. The site includes an ever-changing roster of free advice and craft projects, many involving Dritz dyes.

"DYEING FABRIC" BY CYNTHIA BONNER
http://www.nmia.com/~mgdesign/qor/tech.htm

Here is an excellent introduction to dyeing for quilters, courtesy of Mary Graham Designs. Topics covered include immersion dyeing, direct dyeing, and combination dyeing.

DYE IT BLACK FAQ
http://www.cs.ucl.ac.uk/staff/b.rosenberg/goth/dye.faq.html

A few years ago "gothic" or all-black attire was popular with the hip set. It's still popular with Gloria. Directions for dyeing everything in one's closet black were pandemic on the Internet. "Lady Bathory," a dye shop technician at the University of Tennessee, Knoxville theatre costume shop reveals how to dye just about everything imaginable, including velvets, the blackest black possible. She also covers the use of respirators and other essentials.

"FABRIC DYEING WITH KOOL-AID" BY DAWN DUPERAULT
http://ares.redsword.com/dduperault/koolaid.htm

You read it on the Web first! Exciting new fabrics can be as close as your kid's cup of Kool-Aid.

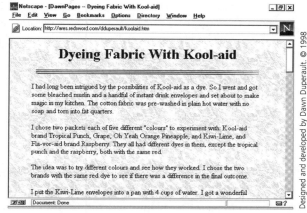

Designed and developed by Dawn Duperault. © 1998

FIBER NEWS
http://members.aol.com/fibernews.html

Fiber News *is a monthly "e-zine"—cyberspeak for an electronic magazine sent to you via e-mail—for fiber-holics: anyone interested in dyeing, or weaving and spinning. The yearly subscription is $10, but you can read many past articles at the Fiber News Web site.*

GRADUATED FABRIC DYEING
http://kathkwilts.com/lessons/dying.shtml

Kathy Somers explains graduated fabric dyeing with Procion fiber-reactive dyes. Be sure to check out Kathy's free cotton candy baskets quilt pattern. It's a beauty!

"INSTRUCTIONS FOR SPECIAL WAYS OF WORKING WITH DYES AND RELATED CHEMICALS" BY PAT WILLIAMS
http://art.acad.emich.edu/faculty/williams/specialdyeinstr.html

More good advice on dyeing from the EMU art department.

🛒 KATHRYN OF THE HILLS' DYE BOOK
http://www.cobweb.net/~ryn/dyebook.html

Fiber artist Kathy Wells offers general directions for dyeing, plus hard-to-come-by information on mordanting wool, dyeing with barks, pokeberry dye and 19th century cheap dyes.

🛒 MENDEL'S TIE DYEING PAGE
http://www.mendels.com/tiedye.html

Mendel's is an art supply and fabric store in San Francisco's Haight-Ashbury—the springboard for "hippie hopefuls," its Web site proclaims. What better place to go for directions, supplies, tips and recommended books on tie dyeing?

🛒 MICROWAVE DYEING
http://www.cottonclub.com/dyeing.htm

The Cotton Club, which specializes in selling cotton fabric (both prints and for dyeing) offers directions on how to dye fabric in a microwave.

"NATURAL DYEING WITH OAXLIS FLOWERS ON COTTON" BY JANIS SAUNDER
http://members.aol.com/FiberNews/janis.html

In this reprint of a Fiber News *article, Janis explains how to dye fabrics with oaxlis flowers.*

QUILTNET ON FABRIC DYE SAFETY
http://quilt.com/FAQS/DyeSafetyFaq.html

Concerned about developing some horrific ailment that only OSHA can diagnose? Read the dialogue of concerns and precautions practiced by QuiltNet members. Another page posted courtesy of Sue Traudt.

QUILTNET ON HAND DYEING FABRIC
http://quilt.com/FAQS/FabricDyingFAQ.html

Here's a nice compilation of messages posted to the popular QuiltNet mailing list discussion group. It includes recipes for using dyes, techniques, supplies, marbling, tie dyeing, and just plain idle comments. It comes courtesy of Sue Traudt's World Wide Quilting web site.

QUILTNET ON DISCHARGE DYEING
http://quilt.com/FAQS/DischargeDyeingFAQ.html

This is the same gabby group discoursing on discharge dyeing, also courtesy of the World Wide Quilting Web site.

QUILTNET ON TEA-DYING
http://quilt.com/FAQS/TeaDyingFAQ.html

Fiber reactive dyes not for you? More interested in dyeing with something safer—say, tea? Read tips on how to do it, courtesy of the World Wide Quilting Web site.

PLASTIC BAG DYEING
http://patchwords.com/dyeing.html

The Patch Words Web site offers directions on how to dye "mess-less" with plastic bags.

PRO CHEMICAL AND DYE, INC.
http://www.prochemical.com/

Pro Chem, a great mail-order source for dyeing supplies, offers lots of super information on its Web site about specific dye lines and how to use them safely and successfully. It also offers Internet-only specials on books and dyeing supplies.

"SPACE-DYEING IN A CROCK-POT" BY GLENNA STANSIFER
http://members.aol.com/FiberNews/glenna.html

In this intriguing article from Fiber News, *Glenna describes how she dyes twisted strands of fiber or fabric in a crock-pot using unsweetened Kool-Aid or Easter egg dye, and mayonnaise jars. By "space-dyeing" she refers to dyeing the fabric so that bands of colors run along it.*

"SURFACE APPLICATION RECIPES FOR PROCION OR OTHER FIBER REACTIVE DYES" BY SUSAN DRUDING
http://www.straw.com/sig/procion.html

Dyeing expert Susan Druding, owner of San Francisco's Straw Into Gold, provides a recipe for a simple technique for printing or spraying Procion dyes onto cotton, rayon, or silk.

"SURFACE DESIGN/FABRIC MANIPULATION: SCRUNCH DYEING" BY CHERYL MCWILLIAMS
http://www.delphi.com/needle/surface2.html

From the Delphi Needle and Thread Web site, this informative article by Cheryl McWilliams reveals recipes, procedures, dye recommendations and tips.

T-NET WEB SITE
http://www.usscreen.com/

You can read over 45 articles on silk-screening on the Web site of U.S. Screen Printing, which sells silk-screening supplies.

THE DECO ARTS WEB SITE
http://www.decoart.com/free/index.html

Deco Arts, makers of a large line of textiles paints, offers free painting advice and project directions.

THE WOAD PAGE
http://www.net-link.net/~rowan/woad.html

This lively Web site, by "Rowan" of the Society for Creative Anachronism, is devoted to the study and use of woad, a blue dye plant used to dye fabrics—and paint bodies—since medieval times. The site includes recipes, techniques, recommended books and suppliers.

 Free Discussion Groups for Quilters Interested in Dyeing

DYERSLIST MAILING LIST

DyersLIST is a free e-mail-based discussion list for anyone interested in dyeing and related surface applications. It's hosted by Pat Williams.

To join send an e-mail message to: **listpro@list.emich.edu** *with the following request:* **subscribe dyerslist** *Your Name. A digest version of the list is available. First subscribe to the list. Then send a second message with the following request:* **set dyerslist mail digest**.

You can read and search a database of all previous messages posted to the list by heading to **http://www2.art.acad.emich.edu/ lists/ dyerslist/search.html.** *Gloria marvels over the treasure trove of information available here.*

Free Rubber Stamping Advice

THE RUBBER STAMPING PAGE
http://www.xmission.com/~jmabunga/stamp.htm

This is one of Judy's favorite places on the Web. John Mabunga's Web site is chock full of great information, tips and FAQ files about rubber stamping, plus lots and lots of links to other rubber stamping Web sites.

 **Why Your Computer Enjoys Multiple Color Realities**
It's a bedeviling phenonmenon, one that is a frequent source of aggravation for artists—the colors on your computer screen are rarely exactly like the ones that come out of your printer. No, it's not because your printer is crummy. It has to do with the physics of how colors are created inside your computer. A simplified version: your monitor creates colors by shooting dots of light, your printer by shooting ink. Read the full explanation at "Color Theory and Pre-Press" by Darren Meyer **(http://cs.wpi.edu/~matt/courses/cs563/talks/color.html)**.

 Free Information on Transferring Photos and Computer Art to Fabric

A REVIEW OF CANON FABRIC SHEETS
http://www.patchwords.com/ofeatures/fabsheet/fabsheet.html

Also from Patch Words, an article on Canon Fabric Sheets—fabric one can print in inkjet printers.

A REVIEW OF CANON PHOTO TRANSFER PAPER
http://www.patchwords.com/ofeatures/phototrans.html

From Patch Words, a review of Canon T-shirt transfer papers for use in inkjet printers.

"BLUEPRINTING" BY DEBRA WEISS
http://www.quiltgallery.com/technique4.htm

An excellent article from Quilt Gallery *magazine on cyanotype, or blueprinting fabric.*

🛒 HANES' T-SHIRT WEB SITE
http://www.hanes2u.com/

Hanes has a wondrous Web site full of lots of tips and tutorials on using T-shirt transfer sheets to create iron-on transfers with inkjet printers. You can use them to make quilts.

HEAVENLY QUILTS FROM INKJET PRINTERS
http://www.execpc.com/~judyheim/qcc1.html

Here's an excerpt from our The Quilter's Computer Companion *on how Canon Computer commissioned three well-known quilters to make quilts using inkjet printers, and how they went about it.*

IMAGE TRANSFERS, FABRIC DYEING AND PAINTING
http://ttsw.com/HowTo/FabricImaging.html

A collection of messages exchanged in the QuiltNet mailing list on transferring photos to fabric, and also fabric painting and dyeing. Compiled by Sue Traudt's World Wide Quilting Web site.

free Quilt History Lessons

One of the most frequently asked questions on the Internet is "How can I restore my grandma's quilt?" The first step is to date the quilt and unriddle the nature of the fabrics she used. Is it a calico from a work apron? Twill from a Confederate soldier's uniform? The second step is to find reproduction and vintage fabrics to patch those worn blocks (if you wish).

Or maybe you don't have an old quilt to repair. Perhaps you're merely interested in the history of quilting—and other needlearts as well. Many Web sites offer articles on quilting history. The articles often include photos of antique quilts and links to other quilting history spots on the Internet. In the next chapter you'll read about Web sites that offer quilt conservation and care advice.

A 19TH CENTURY WOMAN'S PLACE
http://www.digisys.net/users/zsk/welcome.htm

A 19th Century Woman's Place is practically an electronic magazine, with scads of interesting articles on the 19th century woman's role in the home and beyond. Among its fare: articles on the decorative arts, holidays in yesterday and many, many links to other Victoriana sites on the Web.

"A HISTORY OF QUILTING" BY JULIE JOHNSON
http://www.emporia.edu/S/www/cgps/tales/QUILTE~1.htm

This article is from the Center for Great Plains Studies at Emporia (Kansas) State University. It includes a great bibliography.

AMERICAN QUILTS GLOSSARY PAGE
http://www.americanquilts.com/glossary.htm

American Quilts, which sells USA-made quilts, offers a glossary of antique quilt terms. For instance, "popped" refers to a broken thread or a binding not attached in a small place. A "pristine" quilt is one that has not been washed or used. American Quilts also sells "cutter" quilts which are worn quilts that can be fashioned into other things like pillows.

"BLACK HERITAGE VIBRANTLY SHOWN IN QUILTS" BY JULIE STOEHR
http://www.sdsu.edu/daztec/archive/1996/02/08/file005.html

This article from The Daily Aztec discusses how elements of black history are found in quilts.

CRANSTON PRINTWORKS
http://www.cranstonvillage.com/quilt/q-histor.htm

Cranston Print Works, a textile printing firm, offers a brief history of quilting.

DAWN DUPERAULT'S TIMELINE OF QUILTING HISTORY IN AMERICA
http://www.redsword.com/dduperault/timeline.htm

Here's a fascinating page! Dawn traces the history of quilting from pre-colonial Europe into the 1970s. Did you know that in the 1920s blocks colored with Crayons and heat-set were popular? Or that in the 1900s mills perfected the ability to make battings without cotton seed particles stuck in it? Dawn includes an extensive bibliography.

🛒 HAWAIIAN QUILT HISTORY
http://www.poakalani.com/

Poakalani Hawaiian Quilt Designs offers a look at the history of those amazing Hawaiian quilts, plus links to information about Hawaiian traditions and superstitions. This is a truly beautiful site, so plan on spending a lot of time ogling the quilts here.

HISTORY OF SOUTHERN QUILTING
http://xroads.virginia.edu/~UG97/quilt/opening.html

The University of Virginia offers a large repository of articles tracing the different influences found in southern quilts, from European to African.

HMONG TEXTILES
http://www.lib.uci.edu/sea/hmong.html

The Hmong and their beautiful appliqué-and-embroidered quilts are already an integral part of American quilting. Read more about this enticing art, and view some spectacular quilts at this University of California at Irvine Libraries Web site.

HOPI QUILTING: SHARED TRADITIONS IN AN ANCIENT COMMUNITY
http://www.patchwords.com/ofeatures/hopi.html

Read about the role of quilting in the Hopi community, both today and yesterday.

KATHLEEN DYER'S HISTORICAL NEEDLEWORK LINKS
http://www.wco.com/~kdyer/history.html

Kathleen Dyer offers links to a variety of sites around the Internet that offer articles on the history of different kinds of needlework, especially embroidery, lace, and crochet.

"MICHIGAN'S AFRICAN AMERICAN QUILTERS" BY MARSHA MAC DOWELL AND LYNNE SWANSON
http://www.sos.state.mi.us/history/museum/techstuf/civilwar/quiltmag.html

This web page was created by the Michigan Historical Center, Lansing, MI from the article "Michigan's African American Quilters" published in Michigan Historical Magazine, Volume 75, (4): JIA, 1991, 20-23, Authors are Marsha MacDowell and Lynne Swanson of Michigan State University Museum, East Lansing, MI.

MICHIGAN HISTORICAL MUSEUM'S PAINT A QUILT

http://www.sos.state.mi.us/history/museum/techstuf/civilwar/quilt.html

You'll learn about Civil War quilts at this fun Web site, and if you're a teacher you'll find lots of classroom ideas to get your students interested in both the Civil War and quilts that tell its story.

NOTES ON QUILT HISTORY FROM THE QUILTBEE DISCUSSION MAILING LIST

http://needlearts.dm.net/quiltbee/qbqhisto.htm

This is a collection of messages pertaining to quilting history collected from the QuiltBee discussion list (see Chapter 15 to learn how to join the discussion group).

PLANET PATCHWORK

http://planetpatchwork.com/

Rob Holland's Planet Patchwork Web site is well-known among quilters on the Web for serving up compelling articles, many on quilt history. Here are a few:

- *"Civil War Quilt Reveals Deepening Mystery" by Rob Holland*
  http://planetpatchwork.com/cwquilt.htm

- *"A Brief History of the Feedsack" by Jean Clark Stapel*
  http://planetpatchwork.com/feedsack.htm

- *"Buying Old Quilts" by Deborah Roberts*
  http://planetpatchwork.com/buyqlts.htm

RJR FABRICS

http://www.rjrfabrics.com/

RJR Fabrics manufactures many historical reproduction fabric lines well-known to quilters, like the Smithsonian Quilt Fabric Collection, or those based upon fabrics in well-known antique quilts. Its site offers considerable information on the history of quilts, and quilting in particular periods such as the 1930s. Its historical information is organized to accompany descriptions of its fabric lines, so head to those when you tap into this lovely site.

THE LIBRARY OF CONGRESS: AMERICAN MEMORY
http://lcweb2.loc.gov/

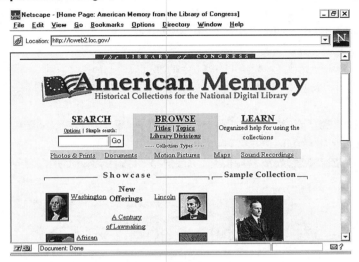

Search on the word "quilt" and this amazing Web site will serve up a list of oral-history interviews with quilters conducted by the WPA work project during the Depression. You can also view photos of old quilts from the library's archives.

THE MINING CO.
http://quilting.miningco.com/

The Mining Co.'s quilt pages, hosted by Susan Druding, offer professionally written and compelling articles each week. Here are some on quilt history:

- *"Molas, Techniques and History of the People Who Make Them" by Susan Druding*
  http://quilting.miningco.com/library/weekly/aa072297.htm

- *"Viewing Antique Quilts Online" by Susan Druding*
  http://quilting.miningco.com/library/weekly/aa100497.htm

- *"Antique Quilt Patterns and History" by Susan Druding*
  http://quilting.miningco.com/library/weekly/aa042797.htm

"WOMAN AND COMMUNICATION: A HISTORY OF WOMEN AND COMMUNICATIONS IN THE 19TH CENTURY" BY LISA BOWES
http://magenta.com/~lisabee/quiltcom.html

Here's an article on 19th century quilting by Lisa Bowes, plus links to other historical sites around the Web. (Take a look at her lovely quilts while you're visiting!)

WOMENFOLK, A GATHERING PLACE FOR WOMEN
http://www.womenfolk.com/

Created by Anne Johnson

You'll find numerous articles about the history of fiber arts, including quilting, on this lovely and welcoming Web site for women by Ann Johnson.The history of the Victorian crazy quilt is explored at:
http://www. womenfolk.com/grandmothers/crazyqu.htm

WORLD WIDE QUILTING HISTORY PAGE
http://quilt.com/QuiltHistoryPage.html

Sue Traudt offers wonderful information on the history of quilting around the world, the origin of different quilting styles, and the stories behind different blocks and techniques.

2 BUSY STITCHING
http://www.2busystitching.com/

This site offers nine "chapters" on the history of embroidery, many including detailed embroidery stitch directions and charts.

 ## Free Quilt History Discussions to Join

 ### QUILTERS' HERITAGE MAILING LIST DISCUSSION
http://www.HickoryHillQuilts.com/qhl.htm

*Hickory Hill Antique Quilts (**http://www.HickoryHillQuilts.com/**), which sells antique quilts as well as a wide variety of vintage and reproduction fabrics for restoring quilts, sponsors a free mailing list discussion group called Quilters' Heritage. The list is devoted to discussing the historical aspects of quilting.*
*To join, send a subscribe request to **QHL-request@cuenet.com**.*
To obtain the digest version send a request to
QHL-Digest-request@cue net.com.
*To post a message to the group, send a note to **QHL@cue net.com**.*
*For more information write **Kris@HickoryHillQuilts.com**.*

Free Information About Quilt Preservation Societies

THE AMERICAN QUILT STUDY GROUP
http://catsis.weber.edu/aqsg/

The American Quilt Study Group, founded by a klatch of quilt historians in California, is dedicated to researching the stories of quilts and quilt-makers. The organization publishes a journal and newsletter, and sponsors seminars.

THE QUILT RESTORATION SOCIETY
http://www.needlearts.com/quilt_restoration_society/index.html

Devoted to helping members restore and preserve quilts, and study their origins, the Quilt Restoration Society hosts conferences and classes, and also publishes a newsletter and journal.

Are You a Garage Sale Hound? Do You Love Riffling through Piles of Old Linens at Estate Sales?

You'll love the Internet fleamarket site Ebay (**http://www.ebay.com**). You can bid on old quilts, old fabric, old sewing notions and patterns—anything you'd find at garage sale, even jars of buttons. It's absolutely amazing what you find for sale at this site—and often for bargain prices.

Here's how it works: You register on the site with your e-mail address. You don't pay anything to bid on items. You can hunt and sift through the Ebay database of thousands of items that are up for auction each day. To bid on an item you enter a minimum bid and a maximum one. The latter is kept secret—unless someone outbids you.

Sales are definitely caveat emptor, since items are offered for sale by individuals around the country, and usually all you know about them is their e-mail address. Are you likely to be fleeced? It depends upon what you bid on. Judy has bought lots of old junk—from vintage clothing to kitschy curtain tiebacks from the '40s. But she usually keeps her purchases under $10. And she would never, ever buy computer equipment from a Web auction site (it's close-out computer stuff on which buyers usually get stiffed). Ebay also offers a reporting feature in which bidders can see comments that other bidders have left about dealers, and one should always read those prior to bidding.

By the way, here's a Web auction tip: Click on the "Ending Today" category to bid on items whose auction ends soon. Most bidders bid on items in the final hours before an auction ends.

 **free** Sewing Machine Help

We quilters love our sewing machines. We use them, collect them, display them in our living rooms and shops. But where do you go when you need help mastering that computerized Bernina? Who do you ask when you want to restore that antique Singer Featherweight? The Internet should be your first stop, for information on cleaning and restoring sewing machines, both antique and new, abounds. You'll find manuals for antique sewing machines available for downloading. You can tap into Web sites of manufacturers like Pfaff and Viking. If you're a fan of antique stitchers you'll find lots of other enthusiasts. Or, if you're merely in the market for a new sewing machine or serger, you'll find advice for shopping.

 ### *Free General Help for Modern Sewing Machines*

 ### AUSTIN SEWING MACHINES
http://www.austinsewing.com/

These Austin, Texas sewing machine stores offer free machine embroidery patterns, a newsletter, and a machine embroidery club.

"BUYING A SERGER" BY ROSE MARIE TONDL AND KATHLEEN HEIDEN
http://www.ianr.unl.edu/pubs/NebFacts/nf93-142.htm

Good advice from a University of Nebraska, Lincoln publication.

PURCHASING A SEWING MACHINE FAQ
http://www.quilt.com/FAQS/SewMachinePurchaseFAQ.html

Another indispensable Internet FAQs, this one from postings on the QuiltNet discussion list, courtesy of Sue Traudt's World Wide page.

RESOURCES FOR LONG-ARM MACHINE QUILTERS
http://www.houseofhanson.com/longarm.html

The House of Hanson offers a list of Web links to Web sites that offer information and advice for long-arm quilt machines, including newsletters, dealers with Web sites, and sellers of supplies.

SEW ASK ME WITH MARTIE SANDELL
http://www.quiltropolis.com/forums/index.cfm?cfapp=25

Have a question about your sewing machine? Ask Martie. Topics include needles, threads, machine talk, and Bernina babbles.

THE SEWING FAQ
http://www.skepsis.com/~tfarrell/textiles/sewing/

Compiled by Tom Farrell and Paulo Ruffino with contributions from the readers of the Usenet newsgroups alt.sewing and rec.crafts.textiles.sewing, this indispensable FAQ contains lots of information on buying a machine, plus advice on pins, patterns, threads, fabric, and free-motion machine embroidery.

WORLD WIDE QUILTING INDUSTRIAL QUILTING MACHINE RESOURCES
http://ttsw.com/Tools/IndustrialMachinesPage.html

Sue Traudt offers this page of information on industrial quilting machines, including a list of instructional videos and manufacturers.

 Free Help for Specific Sewing Machines

BERNINA FAN CLUB HOME PAGE
http://quilt. com/BFC

If you own a Bernina, Sue Traudt's Bernina Club page should be your first stop on the Web. It's full of free sewing lessons, advice, and links, plus a picture of Sue's 1630 Bernina.

PAULA MILNER'S PFAFF PAGE AND FAQ
http://www.cyberport.net/users/milnerwm/pfaffies.html
and http://www.cyberport.net/users/milnerwm/FAQ.html

You'll find lots of links to Pfaff information on the Web, some beautiful embroidery design links, and a FAQ that Paula has compiled from contributions from Pfaffies around the world. She also offers pictures of neat projects that other Pfaff owners have created, and instructions on how they made them.

SUZANNE LANE AUTHORIZED PFAFF DEALER TIPS PAGE
http://www.isn.net/~dlane/tips.html

Suzanne explains lots of stuff: how to keep thread from breaking, "10 Ways to Serger Heaven," how to create thumbnails of patterns, and all the technical advice you crave on the PC Designer software.

JAZZERSTITCHES VIKING EMBROIDERY
http://www.jazzerstitches.com/

Julie Rueckheim offers a huge library of Viking embroidery designs that other Viking owners on the Net have created, and which you can download for free. Hundreds of free stitching designs, like these designed by Martha Emery for the Viking 1+ and Viking embroiders, can be downloaded from the Web. These 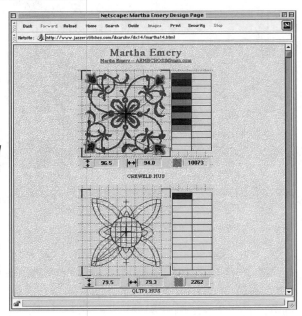 *designs are available on the JazzerStitches Web page.*

 **Create a Quilt Sampler with Your New Home Machine.** The TV series Crafting for the 90s offers a free project lesson on creating a sampler quilt with a New Home/Janome Memory Craft 9000 **(http://www.craftnet.org/c90/newhome/quilt106.htm)**.

 Free Help for Antique Sewing Machines

"ANTIQUE AND VINTAGE SEWING MACHINES" BY ALAN QUINN
http://www.demon.co.uk/quinn/

Alan offers pictures of over 90 different sewing machine models, plus information on shuttle types, like hybrid (transverse/vibrating), oscillating, rotary, plus lots of links to related Web sites.

FEATHERWEIGHT FANATICS HOME PAGE
http://quilt.com/fwf

Find out how to learn the birthday of your Singer. There's also a database of pictures of Featherweights (you can add yours if you wish), and past messages from the Featherweight Fanatics discussion group, all courtesy of Sue Traudt and the World Wide Quilting page.

FEATHERWEIGHT FACTS FROM PLANET PATCHWORK
http://www.tvq.com/fweight.htm

Rob Holland continues on the tradition of the Internet "cult of the Featherweight," as he calls it, with his own collection of facts, stories, and links.

🛒 GAILEEE'S FEATHERWEIGHT SEWING MACHINE INFORMATION RESOURCE GUIDE
http://www.icsi.net/~pickens/

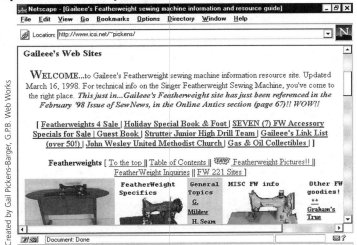

Created by Gail Pickens-Barger, G.P.B. Web Works

the Featherweight Fanatics e-mail discussion group, have compiled a treasure chest of advice on Featherweights, from information on bobbin cases, to oiling, cleaning, and maintenance of belts, lights, and foot pedals.

🛒 BOB BANNEN'S FEATHERWEIGHT & TOY SEWING MACHINES
http://webhome.idirect.com/~bbannen/homepage.htm

Are you looking for a Singer Featherweight, or perhaps a toy sewing machine? Check out this Web site for information and sales.

INTERNATIONAL SEWING MACHINE COLLECTORS' SOCIETY
http://www.ismacs.net

The development of the sewing machine profoundly influenced the growth of quilting. Its invention was one of twists and turns, and nearly a century of diddling by inventors in many countries. (It makes the invention of the computer look relatively simple in comparison.) This site includes pictures and extensive historical information on just about every sewing machine manufacturer that has figured prominently in the past century.

"SUGGESTIONS FOR RESTORING ANTIQUE TREADLE MACHINES" BY DIANE BARLOW CLOSE
http://kbs.net/tt/faq/restoring.html

After digging an old treadle from her neighbor's trash, Judy printed this FAQ and followed its directions on cleaning and oiling. She ended up with a pretty spiffy machine. Gloria is still working on hers!

TANGLED THREADS ANTIQUE SEWING MACHINE FAQ
http://kbs.net/tt/faq/index.html

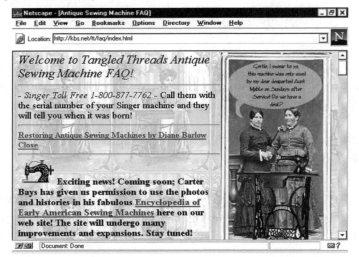

Melissa Bishop and Kapur Business Systems offer fun facts on Featherweights and old Singers in general.

🛒 THE ONLINE ANTIQUE SEWING MACHINE RESOURCE PAGE
http://www2.hawaii.edu/~claw/sew/

Here's a prodigious collection of antique sewing machine info, assembled by Charles Law. You'll find oiling diagrams, extensive links to other Web sites devoted to antique sewing machines, and links to many manufacturers.

 Free Sewing Machine Discussions

E-mail-based sewing machine discussion groups are your very best source of information about sewing machines on the Internet. They're an especially good source for anyone with a high-tech sewing machine. You can get quick answers to questions about just about any brand, and important buying advice when you're shopping for a new model. In fact, many quilters show messages from these lists to their dealers when negotiating prices and features on a sewing machine. You can find out glitches that plague certain models (often before manufacturers admit they exist). You can even get expert help on using those bedeviling memory cards.

PFAFFIES

To subscribe to this free e-mail based discussion list, send an e-mail message to: **majordomo@listserv.embroideryclubs.com.** *In the body of the message type: subscribe pfaffies, or subscribe pfaffies-digest. The latter will bring you the digest version.*

BERNINA FAN CLUB MAILING LIST

Sue Traudt runs this extremely popular list. To subscribe, write to **bernina@ pcnet.com***. In the subject of the message write* subscribe*. Leave the body of the message blank. To subscribe to the digest version instead (a consideration since message traffic on the list is high), write to* **bdigest@ox.ttsw.com***. Write* subscribe *in the subject of the message and leave the message body blank.*

BERNINA 1630

Martie Sandell and Quiltropolis host this discussion group devoted to model 1630s. To join head to Quiltropolis (**http://www.quiltropolis.com**).

BERNINA ARTISTA

If you have a Bernina 170/180 and its Artista software this list is for you. To join, head to Quiltropolis (**http://www.quiltropolis.com**).

DECOLIST

This discussion group, led by Martie Sandell, is devoted to the use of the Brother-made stand-alone embroidery machines. "Its primary focus is to further the creative enjoyment of the BASIC home embroidery machine (with or without a scanner) while forming friendships with fellow owners," Sandell says. To join head to Quiltropolis (**http://www.quiltropolis.com**).

FEATHERWEIGHT FANATICS MAILING LIST
http://quilt.com/fwf

Sue Traudt runs this very popular discussion group for Singer Featherweight fans. The list also discusses other antique sewing machines as well. To join send a message to: **fwf@ox.ttsw.com.** *Write* subscribe *in the subject of the message. If you need help subscribing write to:* **fwfanatics@ttsw.com.**

FREEMOTIONS

Free motion embroidery is the sort of stitching you do when you drop the feed dogs on your sewing machine. Stipling is a form of free motion embroidery, as is free motion machine quilting. To discuss this exacting art with others on Beth Ober's mailing list, send a message to **qlist@quiltropolis.com**, *or head to Quiltropolis* (**http://www.quiltropolis.com**).

INTERNATIONAL SEWING SOCIETY MAILING LIST
http://www.ismacs.net/digest.html

The ISMACS International Digest is for the discussion and sale of sewing machines by ISMACS members as well as non-members. To join you must first read three documents on the ISS's Web site.

LITTLE STITCHES: TOY SEWING MACHINE MAILING LIST
http://www.erols.com/quilts/digest1.htm

Bob Campell runs this mailing list devoted to toy and miniature sewing machines. To join send him an e-mail message at: **tsmguide@erols.com**

LONG-ARM QUILTING

Bona Robinson heads this discussion group, which is concerned with the use and enjoyment of any brand of stand-up quilting machine. To join head to Quiltropolis (**http://www.quiltropolis.com**).

MACHINE EMBROIDERY LIST

To join a discussion group concerned with all aspects of machine embroidery write to: **majordomo@embroideryclubs.com**. *In the body of the message write: subscribe embroidery* Your E-mail Address

NANCY'S NOTIONS WEB SITE BULLETIN BOARD
http://www.nancysnotions.com/

Nancy's Notions runs a Web-based bulletin board where sewers love to discuss their machines. You'll also find on the site products for sewing machines and sergers.

PFAFFERS

This is a discussion group for owners of Pfaff models 1475, 7550, and 7570. It's for busy quilters and sewers who don't want to read a lot of chit-chat. Topics discussed included techniques, accessories, teaching, computer design of stitches and embroidery. To join head to Quiltropolis (**http://www.quiltropolis.com**).

PFAFF TALK

There are two Pfaff Talk discussion groups for Pfaff sewing machines and sergers—one for "hoop" machines like the 7570 and the other for "non-hoop" machines. To join head to **http://www.pfaff-talk.com/**

"PEI'S PFAFF CLUB" NEWSLETTER

For your free copy of PEI's Pfaff Club *write to Suzanne Lane* (**dlane@isn.net**). *Put* "subscribe pei pfaff club" *in the subject line. Please include your e-mail or street mailing address in the text of your message.*

SERGE IT

Lili Fischl and Tina Hoak run this list which is for anyone interested in any brand of serger, either for purchase, everyday use, or embellishment. To join, head to Quiltropolis (**http://www.quiltropolis.com**).

VIKING VENERATIONS

Viking owners chit-chat regularly via this mailing list. To join, write: **majordomo@acpub.duke.edu.** *The body of your message should contain only the words:* subscribe viking-l *(that's an L, not a one).*

VIKING2SEW

Robin Elder runs this list devoted to Viking sewing machines and sergers, and any topic related to customizing, digitizing, and embroidery. To join, head to Quiltropolis (**http://www.quiltropolis.com**).

JAZDOTZ

Julie Rueckheim, hostess of the JazzerStitches Web site (see entry on page 121), runs this list which is devoted to using the HusqvarnaViking #1+ sewing machine and Rose for embroidery. To join head to Quiltropolis (**http://www.quiltropolis.com**).

HUSQVIKING ARTISTRY THROUGH SEWING (HATS)

Lili Fischl and Tina Hoak run this group with discusses all the facets of using the Husqvarna Viking #1+, Rose, #1, 500, and 1100 machines. The emphasis is on embroidery, but other topics like quilting and heirloom sewing are also discussed. To sign up head to Quiltropolis (**http://www.quiltropolis.com**).

Full and Fabulous!

Looking for tips on sewing for full-figured women? Subscribe to the Full and Fabulous Mailing List. For more information head to Quiltropolis **(http://www.quiltro polis.com)** or e-mail list hostess Gail Dennis **(gdennis@ telegram. infinet)**. Gail also runs two other mailing lists: Full and Fabulous Pro, a "no-nonsense" list for advanced sewers; and Full Fashion, which is a fashion discussion group.

Get Free Sewing Stuff by Mail.

Prime Publishing **(http://www.ppi-free.com/freesew.htm)** offers a Web site—and a book that tells you how to mail away for free sewing products like patterns. Most freebies require a stamp or a few bucks for postage and handling.

Bargain-Hunt for Sewing Machines on the Web.

You can hunt garage sale-style for antique sewing machines and collectibles, like old manuals, attachments, and bobbins at the Ebay Web auction site **(http://www.ebay.com)**. You'll find for sale on the site an especially large number of toy and miniature sewing machines. You'll also find lots (and we mean lots) of modern sewing machines and accessories on sale at Mary Field's Sewing Rummage Sale Web site **(http://www.jps.net/cfield/rummage/)**.

WADE'S NEW HOME DIGEST

Peggy and Charles Wade run this mailing list devoted to the New Home sewing machines. To join drop them a personal note at: **wades@norfolk.infi.net.**

Sewing Machine Makers on the Web

Almost every sewing machine maker in the world is on the Web. Their sites are often great sources of tips, tutorials, and free patterns for their machines. They don't usually offer tech support for their machines (alas), expecting you to go to your dealer for that. But if you're having sewing machine trouble and even your dealer can't provide help, sign up for a mailing list devoted to your brand of machine. It's a good bet you'll find the answers in one of the discussion groups for your machine.

BABY LOCK USA
http://www.babylock.com/

BERNINA SEWING MACHINE
http://www.berninausa.com/
http://www.bernina.com

BROTHER U.S.A. HOME SEWING
http://www.brother.com/us-hsm/indexus.html

ELNA SEWING MACHINES
http://www.elnausa.com/

JANOME NEW HOME MACHINES
http://www.janome.com/

RICCAR SEWING MACHINES
http://www.riccar.com/

SINGER SEWING MACHINE CO.
http://www.singersewing.com/

HUSQVARNA VIKING
http://www.vikinghusqvarna.com/

WHITE SEWING MACHINE
http://www.whitesewing.com/

CHAPTER 14

free Software and Computer Advice for Quilters

Interested in trying quilt designing software, but reluctant out of fear that you may not like it? You can download free demo versions of several quilt design programs on the Web. You can also read reviews of quilt software on many Web sites, and find free clipart for use in quilting and craft projects.

 ## Quilting Software Web Sites

AYERSOFT INC.
BARGELLO DESIGNER
http://www.ayersoft.com/

With Bargello Designer you can create beautiful bargello patterns for quilting. The program works with Windows 95 and later, and a demo is available.

CLARIS CORP.
CLARISDRAW
http://www.claris.com

You can download demos of the general-purpose drawing program available for both PCs and Macs.

COMPUTER SYSTEMS ASSOCIATES
V-QUILT
ftp://ftp.clark.net/pub/csa/

You can download a demo version of Phil Hisley's quilt design software for PCs. It's a DOS program, so it will work with any version of Windows, as well as run on older PCs. Click on demovqlt.exe to download the program, and demovqlt.txt to read and print the readme file. To download from this FTP site place your cursor on the file name, right-click your mouse and from the pop-up menu click on Save Link As...

DENEBA SOFTWARE
CANVAS
http://www.deneba.com

You can download demos of the wonderful Canvas general-purpose drawing program, available for both PCs and Macs.

PC QUILT
BY NINA ANTZE
http://www.pcquilt.com/

You'll find demos for both Windows and Mac versions of this quilt designing program, plus sample blocks.

QUILT-PRO SYSTEMS,
QUILT-PRO & QUILT-PRO'S FOUNDATION FACTORY
http://www.quiltpro.com/

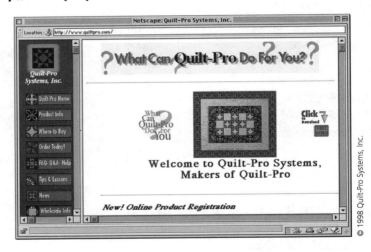

You can download a demo of the quilt-designing software Quilt-Pro, for both PCs and Macs. You'll also find information about the Foundation Factory for PCs (a Mac version is coming), and fabric CD-ROMs. Site also includes patterns and tips.

QUILTSOFT: SOFTWARE FOR QUILTERS
http://www.quiltsoft.com/

Learn about QuiltSOFT quilt design software and fabric disks at the QuiltSOFT Web site. No demos available at present.

THE ELECTRIC QUILT COMPANY,
ELECTRIC QUILT & BLOCKBASE
http://www.wcnet.org/~equiltco/

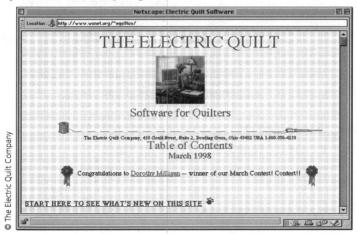

At the Electric Quilt Company's Web site you'll find tutorials on Electric Quilt and Blockbase, plus free art to use on your Web page. You'll find lots of product information, news, patterns—plus free Web graphics. No demos available at present.

Software for High-Tech Sewing Machines

Looking for tips on using software like Pfaff's PC-Designer for creating stitch patterns to download to a computerized sewing machine? Head to Free Sewing Machine Help, Chapter 13, for Web sites that offer advice, links, and even stitches that you can download.

If you use Electric Quilt quilt design software you can join in a mailing discussion group that regularly shares advice. Head to Electric Quilt's Web site (**http://www.wcnet.org/ElectricQuiltCo**) for directions on how to join.

 ## Free Quilt Software Reviews

COMMENTS ON QUILTING SOFTWARE FROM USENET
http://www.redsword.com/dduperault/review.htm

Dawn Duperault has compiled comments and reviews on quilt designing software that quilters wrote in the Usenet newsgroup rec.crafts.textiles.quilting.

PLANET PATCHWORK'S QUILT SOFTWARE REVIEWS
http://planetpatchwork.com/qltprogs.htm

Rob Holland serves up in-depth (and very opinionated) reviews of all the major quilt design programs. You can also read an essay by Catherine Jones, "Distributed Creativity: Speculations on Quilting, Computers, and Art" (**http://www.tvq.com/cathjone.htm**).

QUILTNET COMPUTER SOFTWARE FAQ
http://ttsw.com/FAQS/ComputerSoftwareFaq.html

This is a compilation of comments on quilt designing software written by members of the QuiltNet mailing list, courtesy of Sue Traudt's World Wide Quilting Web site.

SOFTWARE REVIEWS BY BENCHIN' BROWSE
http://www.benchin.com/cgi-win/$br/cat/1402

You'll find reviews of quilting and other needlework software at this popular Web site.

THE NEEDLECRAFTER'S COMPUTER COMPANION
http://www.execpc.com/~judyheim/needle.html

You can read about Judy's book, including an excerpt on how to buy quilt designing software.

THE QUILTER'S COMPUTER COMPANION
http://www.execpc.com/~judyheim/qcc.html

You can read about our book (in which we review quilt software), plus read excerpts.

SOFT EXPRESSIONS
http://home.earthlink.net/~mesa1/

Read about Sharla Hicks' series of Computer Quilting Made Easy books. She offers her views on quilting software packages too.

 ## *Free Clipart*

What can you do with clipart? You can use it to decorate your Web page, turn it into Windows screen splashes and icons, and even use it as the basis of appliqué patterns.

But you need to be careful. Most art in the world is copyrighted —that means that someone owns the image, and you need their permission to use it. Sometimes you need to pay a fee. And sadly the Internet is awash in pirated art, particularly clipart, so you need to be careful where you get art that you use on your Web page, and you often need to ask permission to use it.

Here are some Web sites that offer free clipart for use on Web pages and in Windows icons. Some of the art has been created by the site's owner, some has not. Some images come with restrictions—you can use the pictures on your Web page, for example, but you may need permission to use them elsewhere.

We can't stress it enough: always be careful when you're using someone else's art. Find out where the art came from, get permission to use it. If you plan to use the art in a commercial venture, like a pattern or quilt you plan to sell, get permission in writing.

AUNTIE'S FREE WEB CLIPART
http://www.auntie.com/watkins/main.asp

BARRY'S CLIP ART SERVER
http://www.barrysclipart.com/index.html

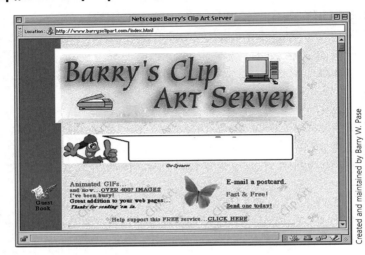

Barry's is one of the largest clip art libraries on the Web.

HOW TO MAKE QUILT ICONS FOR YOUR COMPUTER FROM COMPUQUILT
http://www.compuquilt.com/icons.htm

QUILT ICONS FROM MARY GRAHAM DESIGNS
http://www.nmia.com/~mgdesign/qor/icon.htm

QUILTING ICONS BY NORMAND BOURASSA, COURTESY OF DAWN DUPERAULT
http://ares.redsword.com/dduperault/icons.htm

THE ELECTRIC QUILT COMPANY FREE WEB PAGE CLIPART
http://www.wcnet.org/~equiltco/

CHAPTER 15

free Online Quilting Discussions

Don't have time to join an old-fashioned quilting bee? Hop into cyberspace and join one of the dozens of quilting klatches that swirl through it. Many are just like the quilting clubs our mothers belonged to—members help each other with their stitching, but also share in each others' lives. It may seem improbable, but quilters form deep friendships through their computers. (Our friendship is an example.) More than penpals, quilters get together for quilting shows and shopping trips, they cheer each other on through life's challenges and victories. Some of us can't imagine what life would be like without our quilting cyber-pals. We think that if you're not online already you owe it to yourself to plug in your modem and join the fun.

Best of all, you can participate in these guilds in your bathrobe and slippers—and you don't need to bring a dessert.

 ## Free Web Page Quilt Guilds or Message Boards

Some of the big Web sites for quilters host message boards where you can write and reply to messages penned by quilters around the globe. Delphi's Quilting Arts Forum and the National Online Quilters are the two liveliest—they're essentially cyber-space quilting guilds. Some of these sites are quite marvelous, and offer many things besides good conversation, like patterns and information file libraries, regular feature articles, and guests. Best of all, they're simple to tap into. Once you get to the Web addresses listed below, click the "forum" or "message board" button or link to find the conversations.

DELPHI'S QUILTING ARTS FORUM
http://www.delphi.com/quilting/

Judy Smith hosts this electronic quilting guild extraordinaire. Blocks of the month, message boards, fabric and block swaps, free patterns and more are the fare.

DELPHI'S SEWING FORUM
http://www.delphi.com/needle

Judy also hosts this mega-site where you'll find free patterns, projects, tips, and of course lots of wonderful conversation.

DELPHI'S TEXTILE ARTS FORUM
http://www.delphi.com/textile

Run by Rita Levine, this group discusses just about everything under the moon related to textiles. It has a wonderful library, and lots of wonderful people online.

JO-ANN FABRICS & CRAFTS MESSAGE BOARDS
http://www.joann.com/index.stm

Jo-Ann Fabrics offers lively message boards on a variety of crafting passions, including quilting.

NANCY'S NOTIONS
http://www.nancysnotions.com/

Tap into this Web site run by the Sewing with Nancy people for bulletin board-based discussions of fabric, sewing, quilting, and more.

NATIONAL ONLINE QUILTERS
http://www.noqers.org/

This is an especially lively online quilt guild run by Cheryl Simmerman. You'll find projects, challenges, a library of files to download, like demos of quilting software, and an active message board.

THE ARTS & CRAFTS SOCIETY
http://www.arts-crafts.com/

You'll find some very eclectic discussions on this Web site devoted to the Arts & Crafts movement—topics like block-printed fabrics and Frank Lloyd Wright-style textiles. Be sure to read the archives.

Meet Japanese Quilters

Find out what quilters in Japan are up to.
Head to the Web site of FCREATE, the quilters on the
quilt forum on NIFTY-Serve, the Japanese online service
(http://member.nifty.ne.jp/Gucky/e_index.html). There are no
message boards here (at least not yet) but you can view
their projects.

Trade Blocks and Fabrics with Pen-Pals

Most of the online quilting groups listed in this chapter
conduct regular organized exchanges of blocks and fabric
among members. Sue Traudt's World Wide Quilting Page
offers a "trading post" **(http://quilt.com/TradingPost.html)**
where quilters can exchange blocks and fabrics on a one-
to-one basis with other quilters. Sue also offers a FAQ on
how to set up and run e-mail quilt block and fabric
exchanges. Kathy Somers also offers a page of regular
swaps organized around fun themes like "mythical crea-
tures" **(http://kathkwilts.com/swaps.html).**

Free Quilting Mailing List-Based Discussions

Special-interest mailing lists are where most knowledge is shared
on the Internet. That's true for quilting, and for other subjects as
well. Head to Chapter 1 for an explanation of what a mailing list
is all about. We've sprinkled mailing list recommendations
throughout this book. Here are some general-interest quilting
mailing lists, and details of how to join them.

You should head to the following Web pages to read the directions on how to join the list. In most instances you'll need to
send an e-mail message to a computer that will add you to the
mailing list. It will send you a confirmation message telling you
that you're signed up. After that, any messages posted to the list
will arrive in your mailbox each day.

ART2WEAR, RUN BY EDIE EVANS
http://www.quiltropolis.com

CRAZY QUILT, RUN BY DAWN SMITH AND BETH OBER
http://www.quiltropolis.com

DOLLMAKERS
http://www.everink.com/dm/index.html

THE DOLL STREET DREAMERS DOLL CLUB, RUN BY MOLLY FINNEGAN, LORI SCIANNA, AND VIVIENNE STEWART
http://www.dolltropolis.com/dollstreet/

(A request from the list owners to subscribers: "DO wear a stunning hat while posting.")

DOLLWORK
To subscribe write to: **majordomo@ml.rpmdp.com.** *In the body of the message type:* subscribe dollwork-digest

ELECTRIC QUILT
http://www.wcnet.org/ElectricQuiltCo/Infoeq.htm
(to discuss use of Electric Quilt software)

FRIENDS OF CLOTH DOLLS
http://www.thedollnet.com/friends/

KAFFEE-KLATSCH QUILT CHAT, RUN BY SUE TRAUDT
http://quilt.com/KaffeeKlatsch/KaffeeKlatsch.html

PRO-QUILT, RUN BY DAWN DUPERAULT
http://ares.redsword.com/dduperault/list.htm
(for professional quilters)

QUILTART, RUN BY JUDY SMITH
http://www.quiltart.com/

QUILTBEE
http://needlearts.dm.net/quiltbee/
Another lively group that's easy to tap into through the Web.

QUILTER'S HERITAGE
http://www.HickoryHillQuilts.com/qhl.htm

QUILTER'S ONLINE RESOURCE CONNECTION, RUN BY MARY GRAHAM DESIGNS
http://www.nmia.com/~mgdesign/qor/qorc.htm

QUILTNET
http://sjcpl.lib.in.us/MFNet/MFNetLife/QuiltNetMail.html

QUILTOPIA, RUN BY ROB HOLLAND
http://planetpatchwork.com/quiltop.htm

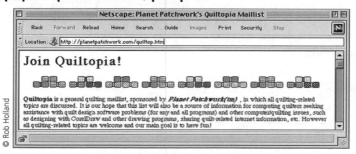

SEWBIZ, RUN BY JUDY KAUFMAN
http://www.quiltropolis.com

SEWPROS NETWORK, RUN BY KAREN MASLOWSKI
http://sewstorm.com/sewpros.htm
(for professional sewers)

THE SEWING LIST, RUN BY JULIE PAGE
http://www.quiltropolis.com

WATERCOLOUR QUILTING, RUN BY MARILYN LEVY
http://www.quiltropolis.com

Mailing List Essentials

When you sign up for a mailing list, you will receive an e-mail message telling you the address you will use to send messages to everyone on the list, and the address for unsubscribing or changing your subscription. These are different addresses. Be sure to print this message and keep it for future reference. Some mailing lists are chatty, while others require members to stick to the topic at hand. Be sure to read the list's rules to find out what kind of conversations are permitted on the list. Commercial posts are generally forbidden in these lists.

Some mailing lists fill your e-mail box with hundreds of messages a day. If that's an inconvenience, subscribe to the list's digest version. The day's conversation will be mailed to you as one long e-mail message at the end of the day.

Never forward to everyone on the list e-mail messages warning of computer viruses. These messages are often hoaxes. If you are concerned about a virus, forward the message to the person running the list.

Don't forward to everyone on the list messages requesting donations for charities or victims of illness or tragedy. Unfortunately, many such messages circulating the Internet are scams. If you believe the message is legitimate and worth consideration, forward it instead to the person running the list.

How To Find More Mailing Lists.
For more quilting mailing lists head to Quiltropolis (**http://www.quiltropolis.com/ NewMailingLists.htm**). The company runs a growing and changing selection of over twenty quilt discussion lists. To search out lists in other interests, head to The Liszt (**http://www.liszt.com**) or The List of Publicly Accessible Mailing Lists (**http://www.neosoft. com/internet/paml**). Literally hundreds of thousands of mailing lists spanning every conceivable topic populate the Internet, including many needlework ones.

Don't Overlook Subscription Mailing Lists.

Several quilting mailing lists require an annual subscription fee, usually from $10-$15. While some quilters balk at paying to join a list, we don't think it's unreasonable to ask a fee. These lists require an incredible investment of time, as well as computer resources to run. We think that the lists that we've paid to join have generally been well-worth their modest fees. Ozz Graham runs a subscription list called QuiltBiz, for discussing quilting as a business. For more information write her at: **ozzg@nmia.com.** Melissa Bishop runs several for-pay mailing lists through her Tangled Threads Web site (**http://kbs.net/tt/groups.html**). They include: InterQuilt (a general-interest quilting list); the Pfabulous Pfaff Pfan Club; Rag Dolls (for dollmakers); and Sew Old (for fans of heirloom sewing).

You're Never Too Old for a Secret Pal.

Several of the quilting mailing lists and Web-based guilds conduct "angel" programs. Quilters are assigned secret pals who remember their birthdays, send them fat quarters and other gifties, and, at the extreme, are directed to "look out" for their charge on the Internet. Who told you fairy godmothers don't exist?

 ### Free Quilting Chat Groups

Chat, or "internet relay chat" is what happens when two or more people carry on a conversation by typing to each other while logged into the Internet. There are several Web sites devoted to conducting quilting chats. Chats often occur on specific days and scheduled times, and may include guests of quilt teachers or artists.

In order to participate you may need to download special chat software, or run up-date-versions of Netscape or Internet Explorer, with Java enabled. The chat's official Web site will fill you in on what you need to do. The sites often have directions on how to join the conversation if you're connecting to the Web via TV. Log into these Web sites for more information and chat schedules.

AUNTIE'S QUILT CHAT
http://www.auntie.com/quiltchat.htm

CANADIAN QUILTERS ONLINE, QUILTER'S ANONYMOUS CHAT PAGE
http://www.barint.on.ca/~wfitzger/cqolhome.html

DOLL STREET DOLL CLUB:
THE CHATTERS' CAFE & CAR WASH
http://www.dolltropolis.com/dollstreet/chatters.htm

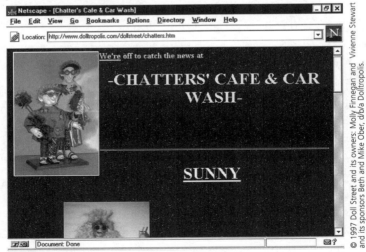

Join in the madcap conversations and adventures at Doll Street Doll Club.

DELPHI'S SEWING CHAT
http://www.delphi/needle

DELPHI'S TEXTILE ARTS CHAT
http://www.delphi/textile

MINING CO. QUILTING CHAT
http://quilting.miningco.com/mpchat.htm

NATIONAL ONLINE QUILTERS CHAT
http://www.noqers.org/

#QUILTCHAT BY KATHY SOMERS
http://www.kathkwilts.com/starchat.shtml

QUILTTALK, SPONSORED BY QUILT MAGAZINE
http://www.quilttalk.com/

This quilt chat channel is devoted to "quilting bee fun."

QUILTROPOLIS CHAT
http://www.quiltropolis.com/

Usenet Newsgroup Discussions

Newsgroups are public discussion groups that you read with your Web browser's news reader. Head to Chapter 1 for directions on how to tap in with your specific browser. In general, quilting and sewing newsgroups are less personable and chatty in tone than mailing lists. (We think they're less fun.) But quilters share valuable information in them nevertheless. Here's a list of newsgroups of interest to quilters:

rec.crafts.textiles.quilting
Anything having to do with quilting

rec.crafts.textiles.needlework
Any form of hand-stitching is discussed

rec.crafts.textiles.sewing
Sewing clothes, furnishings, etc.

rec.crafts.textiles.yarn
Any craft involved with yarn

rec.crafts.textiles.misc
Miscellaneous fiber and textile discussions

rec crafts.marketplace
Small ads for craft products.

 *Help Find Lost Quilts.*
If you're looking for a recently lost quilt, or know of a homeless one that has been found, head to The Lost Quilts Page **(http://www2.succeed.net/~amc/quilts.ht.)**.

CHAPTER 16

free Quilt Magazines

Many quilting magazines host Web sites, where they publish smatterings of articles and patterns from current issues. But in addition to "newsstand" quilting magazines, you will also find on the Web electronic magazines, or "e-zines" in cyber-speak. These are magazines you'll read nowhere else. Some are humble efforts that are distributed via e-mail. Others are lavish displays featuring quilts, hotlinks, and snazzy graphics which put their newsstand counterparts to shame. Here's a guide to the Web sites of both major quilting magazines and quilting e-zines.

Free Web Sites for Newsstand Quilt Magazines

AMERICA'S FAVORITE QUILTING MAGAZINES
http://www.quiltmag.com/

You'll find lots of your favorite quilt magazines on the Web offering patterns, lessons, advice and more. This is the home of Quilt Almanac, Quilt, Miniature Quilt Ideas, Country Quilts *and* Big Block Quilts. *The magazines offer lessons, patterns, and tips online.*

THE CLOTH DOLL MAGAZINE
http://www.theclothdoll.com/

You can read lots of great excerpts including interviews with doll-makers and tutorials like how to make life-like eyes.

DOWN UNDER QUILTS
http://www.duquilts.com.au/

Read what Australian quilters are up to at this marvelous site sponsored by Down Under Quilts magazine. Frankly, we think that all the tips, links, and articles on this site make it the nicest quilt magazine site on the Web.

THE FOUNDATION PIECER
http://www.other-world.com/ftp/quiltersweb/ZippyDesigns/ZTFP/ZTFPindex.html

You'll find pictures of projects in issues and occasionally free patterns.

QUILTS ONLINE
http://www.quilts-online.com/

This is the cyberspace home of Quilter's Newsletter Magazine *and* Quiltmaker. *You'll find monthly block patterns, tip, and articles from the magazines.*

Quiltmaker offers tips and patterns on its Web site.

THREADS MAGAZINE ONLINE
http://www.taunton.com/th/index.htm

Threads offers a wide selection of how-to articles and tips from the magazine.

Find Other Magazines You Like on the Web.
Like we said, just about every magazine runs its own Web site. To find the ones you're interested head to the publication lists of one of the major searchers like Yahoo (**http://www.yahoo.com/News/Magazines/**).
Or, check out these magazine sites:

- ### COUNTRY COLLECTIBLES
  http://www.countrycollector.com

  Read stories from the magazine, plus find craft projects including ones for quilting.

- ### HEARST HOME ARTS
  http://homearts.com

  You'll find all the Hearst home-oriented magazines here including Victoria, Country Living, Good Housekeeping, and Redbook. You can read selections from all, plus special features written for the Web.

- ### MARTHA STEWART LIVING
  http://www.marthastewart.com

  Martha Stewart fans will find show schedules and upcoming news on books and Martha Stewart Living.

Find More Quilt Magazines.
Like fat quarters you can never have enough of them—subscriptions to quilt magazines, that is. When you tire of reading them on the Web subscribe to them by mail. On Sue Traudt's World Wide Quilting page you'll find a "Quilt Magazine FAQ" (**http://ttsw.com/FAQS/Quilt MagazineFAQ.html**) compiled from messages written by quilters on which magazines they like, which ones they don't. It includes a list of addresses and subscription information for quilt magazines. Dawn Duperault also offers a list of quilt magazines and their addresses (**http://www.redsword.com/dduperault/magazine.htm**).

Free (or Nearly Free) Electronic Quilt Magazines

THE DOLL STREET GAZETTE
http://www.dolltropolis.com/dollstreet/gazette5.htm

Here's a lively e-zine for doll-makers run by editor Molly Finnegan. It covers such topics as how to make shaped felt hats for dolls.

FIBERNEWS HOME PAGE
http://members.aol.com/FiberNews/fibernews.html

You'll enjoy this monthly e-mail newsletter for fiber arts enthusiasts by Lili Pintea-Reed, owner/editor. There is a small subscription fee, but a free issue and some articles are available for reading at the Web site.

LET'S TALK ABOUT DOLLMAKING ONLINE MAGAZINE
http://exit109.com/~mimi/letstalk/letstalk.htm#NewProd

Doll-maker Gloria J. "Mimi" Winer and Jim Winer offer book reviews, show information, and photos.

NINE PATCH NEWS
http://members.aol.com/ninepatchn/index.html

From America Online's quilting forum comes a newsletter written by AOL quilters. Topics are chatty and cover topics ranging from use of masking tape to shopping trip experiences. You can read it on the Web site or get it via e-mail.

PATCHWORDS
http://www.patchwords.com/

Patchwords is a fun, homey, and helpful publication that you can read only on the Web. This is a delightful publication assembled by volunteer quilter-editors. Each month Patchwords offers new articles, quilting patterns, tips and techniques, letters to the editor, quilting pen pals and more. Be sure to check out "Crabby Ethel Surfs the Web" for quilting Web site reviews.

QUILT GALLERY MAGAZINE
http://www.quiltgallery.com/

Quilt Gallery is a must-read for quilters on the Web. This is an amazing and beautiful online publication devoted to contemporary quilting. It offers an online discussion area and e-mail notification of new issues. Reading it is free.

QUILTERS' NUGGETS NEWSLETTER
http://quilting.miningco.com/library/weekly/blQNuggt.htm

You can get a free weekly newsletter from Quilting on the Mining Co., hosted by Susan Druding. The newsletter tells you what's new on the site.

QUILTZINE
http://www.auntie.com/qzine/

Auntie-Dot-Com posts an e-zine that includes projects and patterns, and tells you what's new on the Auntie craft site.

THE VIRTUAL QUILTER
http://www.planetpatchwork.com/

Rob Holland writes the most outspoken quilting e-zine on the Web. Get it delivered to your e-mail box for $5 a year. You can read a free issue on the Web site.

 Directories to Help You Give Others a Hand

There's nothing quilters love more than a quilting charity project. Quilters on the Internet are an especially generous bunch, stitching quilts for sick children, disaster survivors, and anyone who needs a helping hand. Here's a guide to some of the quilting and sewing charity projects you can get involved with through the Internet.

ABC QUILTS PROJECT
http://www.jbu.edu/ABCQuilts/index.html

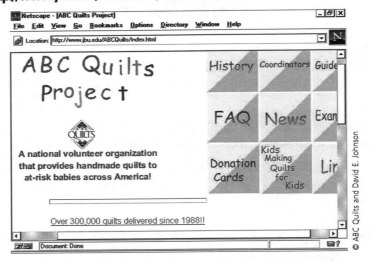

ABC sews quilts for at-risk kids. They have a great program in which kids can make quilts for other kids.

🛒 THE BOISE PEACE QUILT PROJECT
http://www.peacequilt.org/

The Peace Quilt Project is a group of quilters who stitch quilts to give to world leaders and organizations that have made significant contributions in the causes of peace, justice, and the environment.

CARING AND SHARING, FROM THE HOME SEWING ASSOCIATION
http://www.sewing.org/careshare/index.html

You'll find free patterns for items popular with sewing charity projects at the Home Sewing Association's Web site. This wonderful site offers free patterns that are popular with sewing and quilting charity projects, such as "angel" gowns for preemies and chemotherapy turbans. The site also offers a bulletin board for discussing charity projects.

"GOOD WORKS AND CHARITY QUILTING" FROM THE MINING CO.
http://quilting.miningco.com/library/weekly/aa081997.htm

Susan C. Druding, quilting guide for the Mining Co., offers links and information on quilting charity projects.

INTERQUILT'S HUGS PROJECT BEARS FOR KIDS
http://kbs.net/tt/hugs.html

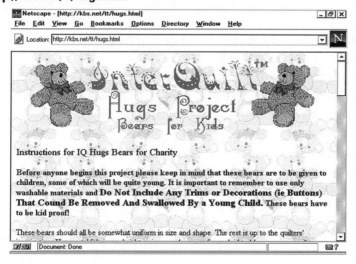

Melissa Bishop's InterQuilt mailing list discussion group sews bears for children in need. Tap in to find out more. They also offer their preferred bear pattern online, downloadable in Adobe PDF format. Also take a look at the Tangled Threads Has a Heart Web page **(http://kbs.net/tt/heart.html)** *for more information and links to quilting charity projects around the Web.*

MANITOBA FLOOD QUILT RELIEF
http://www.dilkie.com/quilt.htm

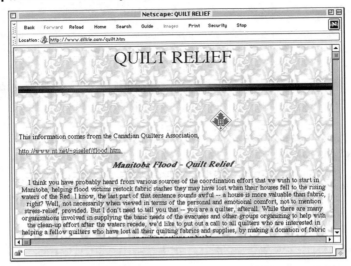

The Canadian Quilter's Association offers help—and hope to flood victims.

THE NAMES PROJECT FOUNDATION:
AIDS MEMORIAL QUILT
http://www.aidsquilt.org/quilt/

You can view the AIDS quilt on this Web site, plus obtain directions on submitting a panel.

PROJECT LINUS, PROVIDING SECURITY THROUGH BLANKETS
http://members.aol.com/blankets/

Project Linus sews and delivers security blankets to children throughout the country undergoing difficult situations.

PROJECT WARM FUZZIES
http://users.accessus.net/~davenkim/pwf/pwf.html

Project Warm Fuzzies sews quilts to give to children at St. Jude's, the twenty-plus Shriners' hospitals, and other hospitals.

QUILTING WITH CHILDREN
http://ariel.ccs.brandeis.edu/~heddi/

Heddi Craft, a sixth grade teacher, describes projects, techniques, resources and stories by, about and for making quilts with kids.

RAGING LIGHTS PROJECT: THE BREAST CANCER NAMES BANNER
http://www.his.com/~judy/ragingl1.html

Susan Gray started a banner quilted with names of breast cancer victims to be carried to breast cancer fund-raising events (the carrying of quilted and embroidered banners has a long history in women's political campaigns). You can learn how to get involved at this informative site.

SEWING WITH NANCY'S SEW A SMILE
http://www.nancysnotions.com/sewsmile.html

Nancy Zieman and Nancy's Notions offer a large directory of charity quilting and sewing projects, many of which can be e-mailed.

WASHINGTON REGIONAL TRANSPLANT CONSORTIUM
http://www.clark.net/pub/wrtc/quilttmb.htm

You can view quilts created by donor families at this inspiring site.

Giving Can Be as Simple as Rummaging through Your Closet.
Many of these charity sewing projects are eager for donations of fabric, batting, and thread. Head to their Web sites to find out what they need.

Yes, Quilting Charity Projects Are Everything in Cyberspace.
Many of the quilt mailing lists featured throughout the book also conduct charity projects. Pitching in can be as simple as getting together with your friends via e-mail.

CHAPTER 18

Information on Quilt Guilds, National Organizations, and Contests

Even though quilters meet through their computers, they still love to get together in person. Many quilting guilds host their own Web pages. Some are austere, offering only membership information, while others are vast networks offering information on upcoming shows, galleries of member's quilts, and information on local shopping (making them good sites to tap into when you're traveling).

Many national quilting and needlework organizations also host Web sites offering information on activities and membership. Lots of quilting contests also advertise through Web sites. We've included at the end of this chapters Web sites that offer directories of these contests.

Free Information on Local Quilting Guilds and Activities

DAWN DUPERAULT'S QUILT GUILDS ONLINE
http://ares.redsword.com/dduperault/guilds.htm

Dawn offers a list of state quilting guilds with links to their Web sites.

DOWN UNDER QUILTS ONLINE
http://www.duquilts.com.au/

Learn about Australian quilt guilds, quilts, quilt-makers, and quilting business Down Under. You'll also find Down Under Quilts, *Australia's first quilting magazine online.*

MICHIGAN QUILT GUILDS
http://k2.kirtland.cc.mi.us/~bergs/quilting/guilds/

Steven L. Berg has put together this directory of Michigan guilds.

MINNESOTA QUILTERS, INC.
http://www.mnquilt.org/

Carolyn V. Peters runs this site for Minnesota Quilters, which includes information about their annual show, their newsletter, plus links to block-of-the-month doings.

QUILTING GUILDS
http://www.quiltbroker.com/guilds.html

The Quilt Broker offers an extensive list of quilting guilds.

QUILTING GUILDS AROUND THE WORLD
http://ttsw.com/QuiltGuildsPage.html

Looking for a quilting guild in your neighborhood? Tap into Sue Traudt's quilt guild directory. This extensive lists covers guilds in the United States, Canada, Europe, and Australia. This site also includes ideas for guild quilting challenges and activities.

VIRGINIA QUILT GUILDS
http://www.vcq.org/guild.htm

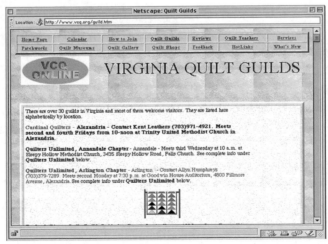

This web page was created by Carol Miller for the Virginia Consortium of Quilters and is supported by the information and pictures provided by its members

Here's a cyber-directory to over thirty guilds in Virginia, plus links to shops, teachers, galleries and more.

THE WORST GIRLS QUILTING CLUB
http://www.wco.com/~carraher/

This Sonoma County, California quilting club boasts hard-quilting, music-loving women. This site includes links to their beautiful quilts.

 ## Free Information on National Guilds and Organizations

THE ARTQUILT NETWORK
http://www.adkey.com/aqn/

Nancy Crow founded this group in 1986, and it now includes 60 members who meet twice a year in Ohio for a three-day retreat. This site offers information on their traveling exhibits.

AMERICAN QUILT STUDY GROUP
http://catsis.weber.edu/aqsg/

The American Quilt Study group, founded by Sally Garoutte, is devoted to the study of old quilts and their stories.

AMERICAN SEWING GUILD
http://www.asg.org/

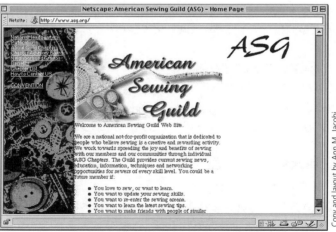

You'll find information here on how to join both national and regional chapters.

AMERICAN QUILTER'S SOCIETY
http://www.AQSquilt.com/

The Web site of this venerable quilting society offers information on membership, shows, and the society's museum.

THE AUSTRALIAN QUILTER'S ASSOCIATION
http://edx1.educ.monash.edu.au/~dtb/aqa1.htm

You can view quilts by members and learn about the society.

THE CANADIAN QUILTER'S ASSOCIATION
http://members.tripod.com/~cqaacc/

Information on publications, events, teachers, and more.

CHARTED DESIGNERS OF AMERICA
http://www.stitching.com/CDA/index.html

You'll find lots of wonderful information here on charted stitching, including lots of illustrations for ribbon embroidery. You can e-mail for information on the CDA.

CONTEMPORARY ARTQUILT ASSOCIATION
http://www.accessone.com/~mesmerie/who1.html

Lorraine Day offers information on the association, how to join, and links to the Web sites of members and their work.

THE CRAZY QUILT SOCIETY
http://www.crazyquilt.com/

The Crazy Quilt Society, a program of the Quilt Heritage Foundation, is devoted to the study and enthusiasm of crazy quilts.

THE CROSS-STITCH GUILD
http://www.greenoff.co.uk/coming.htm

Jane Greenoff tells you how to join the English Cross-Stitch Guild–overseas members are welcome too.

THE EMBROIDERERS' GUILD OF AMERICA
http://www.needlearts.com/ega/index.html

You´ll find information on joining and state chapters, plus excerpts from NeedleArts, the EGA's quarterly publication.

INTERNATIONAL QUILT STUDY CENTER
http://www.ianr.unl.edu/tcd/quilts/homepage.htm

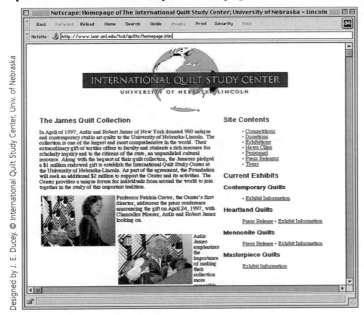

Designed by J. E. Ducey. © International Quilt Study Center, Univ. of Nebraska

IQS, located at the University of Nebraska, Lincoln, promotes the study of quilt-making and traditions. The center also hosts a quilt museum.

THE NATIONAL CRAFT ASSOCIATION
http://www.craftassoc.com/crafttips.html

The NCA offers lots and lots of crafting tips on its Web site. You´ll also find pages on craft show ideas, selling crafts, resources for quilting and sewing, a free newsletter, a chat room, and more.

THE NATIONAL QUILTING ASSOCIATION
http://www.his.com/~queenb/nqa/

You can find out how to join this esteemed society, and obtain information on its annual show.

THE PATCHWORK ASSOCIATION
http://www.paston.co.uk/natpat/natpat

This British organization publishes membership information and links to lists of quilting suppliers and quilting magazines around the world.

STUDIO ART QUILT ASSOCIATES
http://www.saqa.com

Studio Art Quilt Associates is a national organization for art quilters, and also dealers, teachers, curators, and collectors. This beautiful site, created by Jan Cabral, includes membership information and a gallery.

 ## Free Directories of Quilt Contests and Shows

Many quilt shows and contests advertise through Web sites. We couldn't list them all, but here are directories to the ever-changing, ever-growing universe of shows and contests.

JURIED AND NON-JURIED EXHIBITS, CALL FOR ENTRIES
http://www.millcomm.com/~quilt/juried.htm

Carolyn's Home on the Web maintains this directory of juried and non-juried quilt shows and contests. Many of the listings include e-mail addresses and Web links.

QUILTS, INC.
http://www.quilts.com/index.htm#show

You'll find information on the International Quilt Festival, Quilt Expo, and the European Quilt Market.

QUILT SHOWS AROUND THE WORLD
http://ttsw.com/QuiltShowsPage.html

Sue Traudt has compiled this extensive directory of links to quilt shows, contests, classes--and even cruises. She has also included quilt show reviews submitted by visitors to her site.

Help for Lazy Typists

Don't feel like typing a long URL? In modern versions of some Web browsers you can type just the registered domain name of a Web site in order to get to the site. For instance, to get to the American Quilter's Society Web site, you can type **http://www.AQSquilt.com/** or you can type just **aqsquilt**. In Navigator 4.04 or later you can drag and drop a phrase like "American Quilter's Society" to anywhere in your browser's window and Netscape will head out on the Internet and search the major searchers for its Web site. If you drag and drop just one word, though, like quilt, Netscape will treat it as a domain name and, instead of searching the Internet, will take you to **www.quilt.com** (or Sue Traudt's Web site).

 Quilt, Textile, and Fine Art Galleries to Visit on the Web

Nothing is more pleasant than an afternoon spent strolling through an art museum. Museums can provide endless inspiration for quilting projects. But for many of us, the nearest art gallery is a many-hour drive. Now works of the world's masters—including master quilters—are as near as your computer.

We've assembled a list of Web art galleries that we think are particularly interesting to quilters. Some offer images of quilts and other art to view online. Some do not, but we've included them anyway because we think you might like to visit them if you're traveling. We've also included tips on how to use the Web to find information on local quilt galleries when you're planning a vacation.

 ## Quilt Galleries on the Web

Sue Traudt offers a comprehensive list of special and permanent quilt collections on her World Wide Quilting site's museum page **(http://quilt.com/Museums.html)**. This should be your first stop for any museum hopping.

AMERICAN MUSEUM OF QUILTS AND TEXTILES
http://www.folkart.com/~latitude/museums/m_amqt.htm

Although there are no quilts on display here, you can find information on visiting this San Jose, California museum.

ARTS TEXTILE HOME PAGE
http://www.infoform.ch/ArtsTextiles/

This lovely site, which is in German, pictures many modernistic quilts from artists around the world.

THE AIDS MEMORIAL QUILT
http://www.aidsquilt.org/

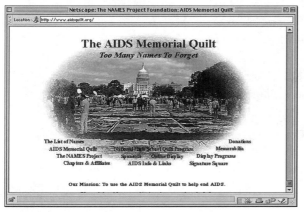

You'll find here a searchable database of over 45 thousand panels that make up the AIDS Memorial Quilt. You'll also find information on exhibits.

THE FLORIDA QUILT CONNECTION
http://www.dos.state.fl.us/dhr/museum/quilts/

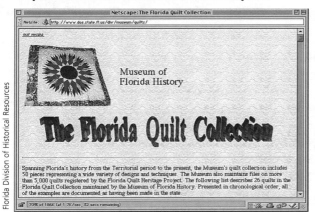

You can view many quilts from Florida's Quilt Heritage Project at the Web site of the Museum of Florida History in Tallahassee.

THE MUSEUM OF THE AMERICAN QUILTER'S SOCIETY
http://www.aqsquilt.com/aqs/maqs.html

The AQS museum in Paducah, Kentucky is every quilter's dream. Find out info on upcoming exhibits and events.

NEW ENGLAND QUILT MUSEUM
http://www.tiac.net/users/mps/

You'll find information on exhibits, workshops, classes and lectures at this venerable museum in Lowell, Massachusetts.

THE PENNY NII COLLECTION
http://www.penny-nii.com/

The Penny Nii Collection is a collector's gallery of "unique arts and global crafts." It features a changing roster of quilt exhibits of private collections that can be seen only on its Web site, like Esprit Corp.'s Amish quilt collection. It also profiles the work of well-known quilt artists like Michael James.

SHARLOT HALL MUSEUM
http://www.bslnet.com/accounts/jccraig/www/quilt.html

You can view the quilts on exhibit at this Prescott, Arizona museum, plus find visiting information.

Quilt Museum Help for Cross-Country RVers!
Planning a cross-country trip—you know, the kind where you stop at every cozy little museum you come across? Artisans, a Mentone, Alabama arts and crafts dealer, offers a list of craft museums by state at their Web site **(http://www.folkartisans.com/pages/nsmusa_d.html)**. The list is reprinted from the book "20th Century American Folk, Self-Taught, and Outsider Art" by Betty-Carol Johanson and Cynthia J. Sellen (Neal Schuman, 1993). Better, buy the book at the Web site.

Never Get Lost on the Road Again
Have trouble navigating the roads of strange cities looking for some well-hidden museum? Plug your laptop into the nearest phone and tap into Vicinity Corp.'s MapBlast **(http://www.mapblast.com)**. Type in the address of where you're located and the address to which you want to go and MapBlast will blast you a street map showing you how to get from point A to B. And it's free!

HEAVENS' EMBROIDERED CLOTHS: ONE THOUSAND YEARS OF CHINESE TEXTILES
http://www.asianart.com/textiles/textile.html

The Asian Arts Web page offers an exhibit of Chinese textiles from the Song, Yuan, Ming, and Qing dynasties.

THE KOELZ TEXTILE COLLECTION, UNIVERSITY OF MICHIGAN (ANN ARBOR) MUSEUM OF ANTHROPOLOGY
http://www.umma.lsa.umich.edu/Orient/Koelz/textiles/textile-exhibit.html

The Koelz Collection at the University of Michigan includes textiles from Iran and Asia. Dr. Walter Koelz assembled this collection of Asian and Iranian textiles in the 1930s. You can see embroidered shawls from Kasmir, turbans from Punjab, and garments from Bombay. (Sorry, the museum does not permit visits.)

THE MUSEUM FOR TEXTILES, TORONTO
http://www.interlog.com/~gwhite/ttt/mtmainpg.html

This is the only museum in Canada devoted exclusively to textiles. You'll find images of a small selection including Nigerian textiles.

THE TEXTILE CHAMBER AT THE MUSEUM OF NATIONAL ANTIQUITIES, STOCKHOLM
http://www.rashm.se/shm/museet/textil/textilkammaren-e.html

You can view Medieval textiles at the Museum of National Antiquities in Stockholm at the Textile Chamber. The museum contains a collection of well-preserved fabric and embroideries from the Middle Ages, most from Swedish churches. It also contains a collection of prehistoric fragments. You can view many of them here.

THE VICTORIA AND ALBERT MUSEUM, LONDON
http://www.vam.ac.uk/

The Victoria and Albert Museum in London has one of the largest textile collections in the world, including many old samplers, tapestries, and laces. It also houses one of the largest collections of Beatrix Potter's drawings, manuscripts, photos and early editions. While not all these are available for viewing on the Web, it appears that some may be making their way to the museum's Web site soon. This is a beautiful site worth frequent visits.

 Free Information on Exhibits at Big Museums with Great Textile Collections

The following museums often display quilts and other textiles. While you can't always view them on their Web sites, you can get information on exhibits.

MUSEUM OF AMERICAN FOLK ART (NEW YORK)
http://www.folkartmuse.org/

THE NATIONAL GALLERY OF ART (WASHINGTON)
http://www.nga.gov/

THE NATIONAL MUSEUM OF WOMEN IN THE ARTS (WASHINGTON)
http://www.nmwa.org/

THE SMITHSONIAN INSTITUTION HOME PAGE
(WASHINGTON & NEW YORK)
http://www.si.edu/newstart.htm

 ### Free Internet Web Art Directories

Looking for work by a particular artist? The best way to find it is by heading to one of the big Web searchers like Excite **(http://www.excite.com)** and typing, say, "Cezanne." Here are some directories that will put you in touch with the world's art. Our favorite is Web Museum Network, run by art zealot Nicolas Pioch in Paris, and mirrored by Web sites around the world. It includes a library of thousands of paintings by the world's masters.

FINE ART FORUM RESOURCE DIRECTORY.
http://www.msstate.edu/Fineart_Online/art-resources/

INTERNET ARTRESOURCES
http://artresources.com/

THE METROPOLITAN MUSEUM OF ART'S WORLD
WIDE ART RESOURCES
http://www.wwar.com/

RESOURCE FOR FOLKLORE
http://miavx1.muohio.edu/~OralHxCWIS/folklife.htmlWEB

MUSEUM NETWORK
http://sunsite.unc.edu/louvre/

More Quilts to See
Don't think you need to tap into the Web sites of museums in order to view gorgeous quilts. Many quilters display their handiwork on their home pages. Surf any of the major quilt Web sites we list in Chapter 2 to find links to many personal cyber quilt galleries.

Help Keeping the Creative Fire Burning

We all need help jump-starting the creative fire at times. Many quilters find that learning and inspiration are two facets of the same process. They learn a new technique, or insight into the world, and that fires an idea. They get an idea for a quilt, and that inspires them to learn new tricks, and the spiral continues. Here's an eclectic grab-bag of sites devoted to the creative imagination.

The Artist's Way

Many quilters are fans of Julia Cameron's book *The Artist's Way: A Spiritual Path to Higher Creativity* (New York: Tarcher/Putnam, 1995). A self-help book for the creative soul, Cameron guides readers through a twelve-week program of journal writing and reflection designed to replace self-destructive habits with productivity.

- **AW-Quilter Discussion Group**
  http://www.quiltropolis.com/

  Quiltropolis runs a discussion group for quilters working through The Artist's Way.

- **Vein of Gold Discussion Group**
  http://www.quiltropolis.com/

  Quiltropolis also runs a quilting-specific study group devoted to Julia Cameron's follow-up book A Vein of Gold: Journey to Your Creative Heart *(New York: Putnam, 1997).*

- **Artist's Way Online List**
  http://www.sff.net/people/Bennefeld/taw/

  You can join a discussion group of artists working through "The Artist's Way" program by heading to this Web site.

- **Artist's Way Web Page**
  http://www.waterw.com/~lucia/aw.html

  Lucia Chambers runs this site for fans of The Artist's Way *that has links to reading groups and member galleries on the Internet.*

 *Worlds of Wisdom*

CREATIVITY WEB
http://www.ozemail.com.au/~caveman/Creative/index.html

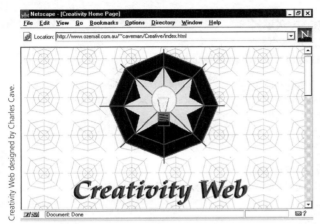

Creativity Web designed by Charles Cave.

Learn about creativity techniques like "mind mapping" and "lateral thinking." Read essays on ways to increase your creativity, and create your own private creative space.

DIRECTED CREATIVITY
http://www.directedcreativity.com/

This self-help page offers the creative new ideas for exploring one's imagination.

DOLLMAKER'S COMMUNITY COLLEGE
http://exit109.com/~mimi/dcc/college.htm

Although this is merely a list of upcoming classes in doll-making taught by doll-artists around the country, the gallery of photos which accompanies each artist and each class description is astonishing.

DOLLTROPOLIS'S INSPIRATION ARCHIVES
http://www.dolltropolis.com/dollstreet/creating.htm

Here's a collection of comments on inspirations posted to the doll-maker's Web site run by Molly Finnegan, Vivienne Stewart, and Abby Cohen-Conn. Now this is one inspired site!

"HOW TO DEAL WITH REJECTION" BY DAVID WALKER
http://w3.one.net/~davidxix/Rejection.html

World-renowned quilt artist David Walker writes eloquently about rejection, how it resonates in one's life, and how to move on.

PLANET PATCHWORK'S
"UNORTHODOX EYES" ESSAYS
http://www.planetpatchwork.com/vector2.htm

Rob Holland's Planet Patchwork serves up a unique collection of essays chronicling, in his words, the "unorthodox opinions of quilters who have looked at quilting through different eyes, and come back to tell us what they saw." Visit often for the essays change frequently.

QUILT DESIGNS USING MATH
http://www2.polarnet.com/~rcoghill/design.html

Julie Coghill offers a selection of intriguing essays and ideas on designing quilts with numbers and through random selection of colors and fabric. She also offers essays on creativity.

THE WEBSTITCHER'S SOURCEBOOK
http://home.earthlink.net/~rcausbrook/index.html

R. Causbrook's beautiful site offers lots of images of quilts and other needlework, plus links around the Web to other sources of inspiration.

More Tips for Searching for Quilting Stuff on the Web

Throughout this book we offer tips for searching for more quilting Web sites and discussion groups on the Internet. Searching for information is surprisingly easy on the Web. In most instances all you need to do is to head to one of the big searchers like Excite **(http://www.excite.com)**, AltaVista **(http://www.altavista.digital.com)**, or Hotbot **(http://www.hotbot.com)** and type a few keywords. Here are more tips for making your searching faster at these big search sites:

Try Different Search Engines—Every big search site is slightly different. Didn't find what you were looking for at Altavista? Try Hotbot.

Try Wildcard Characters—When a search site asks you to enter a keyword to search, try entering wildcard characters to broaden your search. For instance, instead of "quilt" typing "quilt*" will bring up pages that contain words like "quilting" and "quilts."

Try Dejanews—Dejanews **(http://www.dejanews.com)** is a search site that lets you search Usenet newsgroups and mailing lists as well as Web sites.

Follow Links—All you need to find is one or two Web sites that are related to your search topic to go skuttling around the Web to find other closely-related sites. Just follow their links.

Bookmark Interesting Sites—This may seem obvious, but it's easy to forget to bookmark interesting URLs with your browser as you're hopping from one quilting Web site to another. If you ever find yourself scratching your head saying "Wait a minute. Where was that cool web site I visited thirty minutes ago?" use your browser's history feature or drop-down history list to find a record of the URLs you visited.

ABOUT THE AUTHORS

Judy Heim

has been an avid needlecrafter for thirty years. She writes a regular column for *PC World* magazine, and she has written other articles for *Family Circle, C/Net, Newsweek, PC/Computing, Cosmopolitan,* and needlework magazines such as *Quilter's Newsletter* and *Sew News*. She is the author of four other books on needlecrafting and the Internet. Judy lives in Madison, Wisconsin.

Gloria Hansen

has won significant awards for her quilts, most of which were designed using a Macintosh computer. She has written articles for computer magazines (including *Family Circle* and *PC World)* and for quilting magazines (including *Art/Quilt Magazine* and *McCall's Quilting*); she also writes the "High-Tech Quilting" column for *The Professional Quilter*. She has self-published patterns and her quilts have appeared in numerous magazines, books, and on television. With Judy, she is co-author of *The Quilter's Computer Companion*. Gloria lives in central New Jersey.

BIBLIOGRAPHY

Heim, Judy and Gloria Hansen, The Quilter's Computer Companion, *No Starch Press, San Francisco, CA, 1998*

Heim, Judy, The Needlecrafter's Computer Companion, *No Starch Press: San Francisco, CA, 1995*